The Church and People with Disabilities:

Awareness, Accessibility, and Advocacy

Peggy A. Johnson

The Church and People with Disabilities: Awareness, Accessibility, and Advocacy
by Peggy A. Johnson, with Glossary by Lynn Swedberg.
© 2014 United Methodist Women. All rights reserved.

Material from this book not exceeding one-half of published content may be reproduced without adaptation for non-commercial purposes provided the following notice appears with the excerpted material: "From *The Church and People with Disabilities: Awareness, Accessibility, and Advocacy* © 2014 United Methodist Women. All rights reserved. Used by permission." Copyrighted material within the book cannot be reproduced without permission from copyright holder.

For all other requests, contact:
Director of Mission Education and Enrichment
United Methodist Women
475 Riverside Drive, Room 1504
New York, NY 10115
Fax: (212) 870-3695
Phone: (212) 879-3745

All biblical quotations, unless otherwise noted, are from the New Revised Standard Version (NRSV) of the Bible, copyright ©1989, by the Division of Christian Education of the National Council of Churches of Christ in the United States of America. Used by permission. All rights reserved.

Biblical quotations marked KJV are from the King James or Authorized Version of the Bible.

All quotations from *The Book of Discipline of The United Methodist Church—2012*, copyright © 2012 by The United Methodist Publishing House. Used by permission.

ISBN: 978-1-940182-00-1
Library of Congress Control Number: 2013953977
Cover design: Emily Miller
Design: Kellie Green

Printed in the United States of America

United Methodist Women PURPOSE

The organized unit of United Methodist Women shall be a community of women whose purpose is to know God and to experience freedom as whole persons through Jesus Christ; to develop a creative, supportive fellowship; and to expand concepts of mission through participation in the global ministries of the church.

The Vision

Turning faith, hope and love into action on behalf of women, children and youth around the world.

Living the Vision

We provide opportunities and resources to grow spiritually, become more deeply rooted in Christ and put faith into action.

We are organized for growth, with flexible structures leading to effective witness and action.

We equip women and girls around the world to be leaders in communities, agencies, workplaces, governments and churches.

We work for justice through compassionate service and advocacy to change unfair policies and systems.

We provide educational experiences that lead to personal change in order to transform the world.

About the Cover

Most of the symbols on the cover were developed by the Graphic Artists Guild with the goal of promoting and publicizing accessibility for people with disabilities. These symbols are available to download through their website[1] or from other sites where indicated.

The Braille symbol indicates that printed material is available in Braille, including bulletins, hymnals, the Bible, and other publications. This also means that facility signage includes embossed Braille per the ADA guidelines.

The eye symbol indicates programmatic access for people with low vision, such as provision of large print bulletins or audio-taped Bible study materials.[5]

The brain symbol indicates accessible information content is provided for people with intellectual disabilities, including autism, dyslexia, learning disabilities, dementia, and some mental health conditions. Access could include use of shorter words, graphics, and highlighting of the main points.[2]

The companion symbol indicates that personal assistance is available for a person needing physical guidance, for example someone with low vision.[6]

The cane symbol indicates physical access for people with blindness or low vision, which includes tactile markings and elimination of overhead and protruding hazards.

The symbol showing two hands signing indicates that sign language interpretation is provided for the worship service, classes, films, performances, conferences or other programs as well as for meetings and social events.

The harnessed dog symbol indicates access and welcome for people with service animals, such as having a designated outdoor area where animals be can be taken to relieve themselves.[3]

The text telephone/teletypewriter (TTY) symbol indicates the presence of a device used with the telephone for communication between persons who are hearing and persons who are Deaf, hard of hearing, or have speech that is difficult to understand.

The ear with "T" symbol is placed outside rooms such as a sanctuary that are equipped with assistive listening systems.[4] These systems, including FM, loop, or infrared, transmit amplified sound via hearing aids, headsets, or other devices.

The wheelchair symbol indicates access for individuals with limited mobility, including wheelchair users, and is used only where a person can access parking, the building entrance, the sanctuary, and restrooms.

However, in our research to create an appropriate cover design we learned that the disability community is not of one mind (of course!) when it comes to the use of these symbols. Some view them as evidence of progress when it comes to accessibility, others view them as signs of oppression.

Perhaps the best-known symbol of accessibility is the wheelchair icon, known globally as the International Symbol of Access (ISA). It is also the most controversial. The Accessible Icon Project (AIP) has sought since 2009 to transform the old ISA into an active, engaged image. With the permission of the AIP we have used this new symbol on the cover overtop the old ISA symbol to try to convey the complexities of the issue. Please visit the AIP website for more information, to download the symbol for free, and to order stickers or parking lot stencils.[7]

Contents

Foreword 1

Introduction 3

Chapter 1: Awareness 5

Chapter 2: The Bible and Disabilities 7

Chapter 3: Labels and Etiquette 15

Chapter 4: Deaf Culture 19

Chapter 5: Hard of Hearing and Late-Deafened 23

Chapter 6: Vision Loss 27

Chapter 7: Mobility Challenges 31

Chapter 8: Cognitive/Intellectual/Developmental Disabilities 35

Chapter 9: Mental Health 39

Chapter 10: Family Issues and Long-term Support 43

Chapter 11: Veterans with Disabilities 47

Chapter 12: Ordained Ministry 51

Chapter 13: Conclusion and Commencement 55

Endnotes 59

Bibliography 67

Appendix A: Glossary 73

Appendix B: Resources 79

About the Author 82

Foreword

As the father of a daughter with developmental disabilities, I have developed a lot of experiential expertise on what it means to assist someone you love through the maze of challenges that face any person who falls outside of society's definition of normal. Attitudes range from disregard to disdain. Social structures are keyed to exclude or present barriers to persons living with disabilities. I learned how to challenge and overcome these attitudes and structures in behalf of my daughter's right to live the fullest life possible. In the process I gained enormous respect for the parents, teachers, social workers, and advocates who worked to expand and normalize opportunities for my daughter and her marvelously diverse group of friends living with various disabilities.

But it was Peggy Johnson, more than any other single individual, who made me realize how poor the church's record was on ministry with and for persons with disabilities. This is somewhat embarrassing to admit, because I am an ordained elder in The United Methodist Church and have been a theological educator for my entire adult life. It should have seemed obvious to me that persons with disabilities are largely missing or invisible in the life of most local congregations.

Peggy Johnson came to Wesley Theological Seminary, where I taught Old Testament and later became the dean, in order to pursue a Doctor of Ministry degree and to begin teaching for us as an adjunct faculty member. She was already the pastor of Christ United Methodist Church of the Deaf in Baltimore when I met her, and she began to teach courses for us in Ministry with the Deaf and in Ministry and Disabilities. She is responsible for several generations of students sent out into ministry better equipped to minister to and with the whole people of God.

As we became friends and closer colleagues, I became more aware of all the many forums where she tirelessly promoted ministries that would not exclude or ignore persons with disabilities. She taught many, including myself, that we are also missing the gifts of ministry that persons with disabilities have to give, and the witness of the church is the poorer for it.

Peggy became my conversation partner as Wesley joined with those asking why theological education did not include better preparation for pastors and church leaders to extend ministry to God's children with disabilities. Wesley sponsored and hosted the first conference on theological education and disability that expanded to a number of other such conferences around the country. Ultimately, it was my privilege to serve on the team that drafted the first-ever policy on Theological Education and Disability that was adopted by the Association of Theological Schools.

This is so characteristic of Peggy Johnson. She throws pebbles into the pond of our individual, social, and ecclesiastical consciousness and then watches the ripples extend to unexpected places. When she was elected a bishop in our church (and I had the privilege of voting for her), I rejoiced, because I knew this just gave her a higher platform where she could throw pebbles into more ponds. And I was right. I've been present to see her toss a few and the consciousness of the church has been changed by the ripples.

You are about to read the latest of her pebbles. It's coming your way and if you read this book and take it seriously the ripples will change you, and your congregations, and your ministries. You have a treat in store, but you will be challenged as well. It's about time.

—**Bruce C. Birch**
Dean and Professor of Biblical Theology
Wesley Theological Seminary, Washington, DC

Introduction

One of my earliest memories as a child is of taking the bus to Baltimore City with my mother to visit the "Bowen and King" office. I was born with an underdeveloped left eye, medically known as microophthalmia, and since the age of two I have worn an artificial eye. Bowen and King was a company that sold glasses and prosthetic eyes, located in one of the upscale buildings on North Charles Street. Although these trips downtown felt important, there was something tense about them as well. Even as a very young child I could feel that my prosthetic eye was a source of sadness for my mother and it was best not to ask too many questions about it.[1]

After what seemed like hours of waiting in the Bowen and King office reception area, we would be called into a small back room where a tall man, wearing a white lab coat would hoist me onto a gigantic black leather examining chair. The man in the coat would look intently at my plastic eye and then lift it out of the socket with a little red rubber stopper. Then he would open these amazing metal drawers that held hundreds of plastic eyes. They appeared to me like many dismembered people crowded into a drawer. Each drawer had a different eye color. My other eye was something of a bluish gray color. The doctor and my mother would pick out the one that was the best match and the same red rubber stopper would put the new prosthesis in place. It would then be polished and adjusted several times in order to get the proper fit. When the doctor and my mother were finally satisfied, we took the long bus ride back home.[2]

When I was older we went to an ocularist, who would actually pour a mold of my eye socket, paint a bluish gray iris on a little black disc, and create a custom prosthesis. I have had at least twenty "eyes" through the years, as they wear out with time.

Being blind in one eye and wearing a prosthetic eye has given me an affinity with people with disabilities throughout my life. Although everything else in my life and my physical health was normal, I always felt different because of this curious little plastic sliver that sat overtop my underdeveloped eye. I remember being teased in elementary school for being cross-eyed and hearing rude questions by classmates about my glass eye. I often imagined what it would be like to see with two eyes and I wondered why God chose me to be born this way. I have never known the medical reason for my microophthalmia. The most any doctor could say was the condition might have been caused by a virus, and that I should be grateful it affected only one eye and not both.[3]

I believe that my connection with the people with disabilities was the reason why it was "love at first sight" the first time I saw a choir of **Deaf** people signing the "Hallelujah Chorus" at a session of annual conference. I was working as a vocal music teacher in the Baltimore County school system at the time. I was mesmerized by the graceful motions of the words and marveled at the power of the music performed by the hands and arms of people who could not hear it. I vowed that very night that I would learn sign language. Within a few months I began studying American Sign Language at the Christ United Methodist Church (UMC) of the Deaf, the church with the signing choir that I had seen at annual conference.[4]

During that season in my life, I also answered a compelling call to enter the ordained ministry, a call that had tugged at me a number of times during my younger years. When I finally said "yes" to the call to ministry and went off to Kentucky to Asbury Theological Seminary, I thought how wonderful it would be to someday become the pastor of an all-Deaf church. Little did I know that I would later serve the church whose members first taught me their language. During the twenty years I was the pastor of Christ UMC of the Deaf in Baltimore, Maryland, I not only walked alongside people who were deaf but I was privileged to minister with pastors with hearing loss. I also had regular contact with people living with many different challenges, including physical, intellectual, and emotional disabilities. I experienced the church at its best and at its worst as it attempted to minister to and with people with disabilities.

The intent of this book is to build awareness in the church regarding issues around **disability**, to call the church to provide full **accessibility** to services and opportunities, and to promote **advocacy** for justice for people with disabilities. Unlike other categories of human experience, disability crosses all lines of gender, orientation, ethnicity, socioeconomic position, age, and culture. People with typical bodies can be thought of as **temporarily able-bodied** because disabilities can happen at any time to anyone. Therefore, disability should be important to everyone, yet few churches have an intentional ministry or outreach with persons with disabilities.

It is clear to me as a United Methodist bishop with a balcony view of this inclusive, social-justice-loving and faith-filled denomination that we could find ways to improve our ministry with people with disabilities in order to make more disciples of Jesus Christ. As a church, we have yet to experience the fullness of Spirit-given gifts that persons with disabilities can offer when integrated in our ministries. May this book encourage you to identify ways that your church can do more to open the floodgates to **inclusion** and equality.

I commend United Methodist Women for choosing this important topic for their mission study. In the United States and across the globe, United Methodist Women members are engaged in mission work with people with disabilities. Examples of these ministries are described in this book, and a list of United Methodist ministries appears in Appendix B.

—**Bishop Peggy A. Johnson**
Philadelphia Area
The United Methodist Church
Valley Forge, Pennsylvania

Chapter 1
Awareness

Rev. Mitch Galloway has been a United Methodist minister in the Susquehanna Annual Conference since 1980. At age thirteen he was diagnosed with a brain tumor and the necessary life-saving surgery left him without sight. His disability has not deterred him from being an effective minister, but along the way he has experienced obstacles, most of which stemmed from **handicapist** attitudes. When he was first exploring a call to ministry, people told him that "blind people can't be ministers" and questioned how he could conduct a funeral or a baptism if he could not see.[1] In every pastorate he has served during the past thirty-plus years of ordained ministry, Galloway demonstrated that he could carry out every role that a sighted pastor performs. He stated that "it has been my experience that congregations, much like individuals, go through a process of emotional and intellectual changes that culminates in the acceptance of a person with a disability. This process begins with awareness, moves to adjustment and finally to acceptance."[2]

Awareness is the first step toward action. **Attitudinal barriers** can be the biggest roadblock to the acceptance of people with disabilities as whole people who are equal to able-bodied people in every way. As the body of Christ becomes knowledgeable about the realities that relate to disabilities, it can respond to the call of Christ to create accessible congregations and faith communities. These communities will ultimately be stronger when they empower this unique and gifted group of people that make up the largest minority group in the world.[3]

Demographics

Disability issues touch everyone as disability is a part of the human condition. According to the *World Report on Disability*, "Almost everyone will be temporarily or permanently impaired at some point in life. . . . This issue will become more acute as the demographics of societies change and more people live to an old age."[4] Based on 2010 population estimates there are over a billion people on earth living with disabilities.[5] In the United States there are an estimated 54 million people with physical or cognitive disabilities, which is approximately one person in five. Twenty-eight percent have less than a high school education, compared with 12 percent of people without disabilities. Only 46 percent of working-age adults with disabilities are employed, versus 84 percent of nondisabled persons.[6]

The Church and People with Disabilities

Historically, both church and society tended to treat persons with disabilities as objects of charity and kept them out of sight at home or in institutions. Rather than continuing the more recent focus on medical diagnoses and related impairments, the current social model approach addresses the fact that the impact of disability is lessened when social and environmental barriers are reduced. When **handicapping conditions** are eliminated, people with disabilities can take their rightful places in the community.[7] Thus inclusion becomes a human rights issue and the church can be a part of this liberating movement as it lives out the gospel that proclaims justice for all people.

The United Methodist Social Principles make clear that United Methodists support inclusion.

> We recognize and affirm the full humanity and personhood of all individuals with mental, physical, developmental, neurological, and psychological conditions or disabilities as full members of the family of God. We also affirm their rightful place in both the

church and society. We affirm the responsibility of the Church and society to be in ministry with children, youth, and adults with mental, physical, developmental, and/or psychological and neurological conditions or disabilities whose particular needs in the area of mobility, communication, intellectual comprehension, or personal relationships might make more challenging their participation or that of their families in the life of the Church and the community. We urge the Church and society to recognize and receive the gifts of persons with disabilities to enable them to be full participants in the community of faith. We call the Church and society to be sensitive to, and advocate for, programs of rehabilitation, services, employment, education, appropriate housing, and transportation. We call on the Church and society to protect the civil rights of persons with all types and kinds of disabilities.[8]

Despite our affirmation, fewer people with disabilities attend church than able-bodied people. People with more severely disabling conditions are even less involved in the ministry of the church.[9] And sadly, the church is a place where people with disabilities who do attend often experience stares, rejection, and bad theology.

In one of my earliest pastoral appointments there was a young adult with Down syndrome who regularly attended the church. He was a delightful person who participated fully in congregational worship and the outreach ministries. One Sunday a guest evangelist came to the church to preach. At the end of the service he asked everyone to gather around this young man and pray for him. We all cautiously agreed, but were horrified when the pastor prayed for the "demon of disability" to be removed from this young person. This was hurtful and demeaning for the individual as well as his family. The good intentions of the evangelist were fraught with misinformation and a narrow theological perspective.

Rev. Evy McDonald, a United Methodist pastor who recently served in the New York Annual Conference, grew up with disabilities related to having polio as a child. She recalls the pain she experienced when she was not allowed to attend church camp because of fear and prejudice. She left the church for a good part of her adult life because of this rejection.[10]

Churches won't be making these mistakes if they become aware of the needs and the issues related to disability access. People of faith should prayerfully study the Scriptures and learn about the challenges that able-bodied people pose for people with disabilities. A good place to begin improving awareness is to conduct an **accessibility audit**.[11] A thorough survey of the congregation's facilities and attitudes will help identify the specific areas of concern the church needs to address as it reaches out to people with disabilities. As awareness grows, so will the church's heart for outreach. The opportunities for new and expanded ministries are many.

Chapter 2
The Bible and Disabilities

The Scriptures have much to say about people with disabilities. We can also find examples and guidance regarding ministry with people with disabilities. I would suggest that there are three major themes from the Bible that the church should consider as it seeks direction from the Lord in the area of **disability ministry**: healing, inclusion, and **empowerment**.

Healing

When I taught religious education classes to deaf children at a state residential school for the deaf, I met a child who did not want to be there. She was born with normal hearing but at the age of five became totally deaf from a bout with meningitis. This girl did not want to be a student at the deaf school living far from home. She was angry about the sudden onset of deafness that set her life on a radically different path. She told me that she prayed every night for God to restore her hearing, but every morning when she woke up she was still deaf. It was difficult to explain to her why Jesus would not heal her. She had learned many Bible stories about the healing ministry of Christ and felt that these stories held empty promises. Jesus did not heal everyone who was disabled during his time on earth, nor does he do so now. However, miraculous healing is often sought as the answer for those with disabilities.

Most of the people with disabilities in the Bible are found in the healing narratives, especially during the ministry of Jesus who enabled people to walk (John 5), see (John 9), hear (Mark 7), and be restored to mental health (Mark 5), to name a few. When John the Baptist sent his disciples to ask if Jesus was the Messiah, Jesus responded in the affirmative by pointing to the signs of the reign of God that was being ushered in through these acts of physical healing (Matthew 11:2-5). It is arguably true that the Spirit of God brings restoration, wholeness, healing, and peace, then as well as today.

There are other biblical healing narratives. In the Hebrew Scriptures, the prophet Elisha (2 Kings 4:18-37; 2 Kings 5:1-14) performed healing miracles. In the Book of Acts, some people were healed by early church leaders (Acts 3:1-9; 28:7-9). Other accounts tell of persons with disabilities in the Scriptures who were not healed. These include, among others, Mephibosheth (the son of King David's deceased friend, Jonathan), who was unable to walk (2 Samuel 9:1-13); Zacchaeus, who was challenged with a short stature (Luke 19:1-10); and the apostle Paul, who had a "thorn in the flesh" (2 Corinthians 12:7b-10). God worked in the lives of these people as well, not in spite of, but because of their disabilities.

Sin and disability are often connected in the biblical accounts of healing. Jesus told the man whom he cured at the Pool of Beth-zatha, "You have been made well! Do not sin any more, so that nothing worse happens to you" (John 5:14). However, Jesus dismissed disability as a punishment for sin when his disciples asked him whose sin caused a certain man to be born blind (John 9:2). He taught them, "Neither this man nor his parents sinned; he was born blind so that God's works might be revealed in him" (John 9:3).

A Disability Perspective on Healing

Dr. Amos Yong, in his book *The Bible, Disability and the Church: A New Vision of the People of God*, calls us to view the many healing texts from a disability perspective rather than what he calls a **normate** perspective. Reading the Bible from a normate perspective means relating to texts from an able-bodied point of view that equates disability with sin. This viewpoint sees disability as always negative and healing as the answer that ushers in light and life.[1] He continues:

> A disability perspective would thus call into question the normate readings of these biblical texts and illuminate how these have traditionally functioned to oppress people with disabilities. . . . The goal is to be more intentional about observing how the Bible can be redemptive for people with disabilities, despite the implications that any surface (normate) reading of the text suggests.[2]

The disability perspective casts a new and important viewpoint on the meaning of life and does not accept disabilities as a punishment for sin. Disability often brings vitally important insights to all.

The late Reverend Gary Petrillo, a member of the New York Annual Conference, experienced a devastating accident that left him paralyzed and unable to speak. Bishop Jane Middleton recalls visiting the pastor when she was serving as his district superintendent. Through the method of communicating with a letter-board he told her, "You have to lose your life to find it."[3] Petrillo found many ways to be in ministry as a person with a disability that led to a new calling for his life. Disabilities bring a treasure trove of experiences that inform the people of God of the amazing ways that God can work through disability. The church therefore should strive to eliminate moral judgment from the experience of disability.

Faith and Healing

The relation of healing to a person's faith is another scriptural issue that can be interpreted in a number of ways. In the Gospel of Luke (8:43-48) is the account of a woman with a bleeding disorder who reached out to Jesus while he was passing through the crowd. She touched the fringe of his garment and was instantly healed. Jesus perceived that healing power had gone forth from him and, when he inquired as to who touched him, the woman testified to her miraculous healing. Jesus said to her, "Daughter, your faith has made you well; go in peace" (Luke 8:48). Her faith was a key factor in her healing. When the apostle Paul was in Lystra, he came upon a man who had been unable to walk from birth. Acts 14:9b-10 says, "And Paul, looking at him intently and seeing that he had faith to be healed, said in a loud voice, 'Stand upright on your feet.' And the man sprang up and began to walk." The faith of the man with the disability was one of the criteria for his healing.

However, it is also true that even with great faith sometimes people are not healed. I attended a healing service when I was a young adult and asked to receive sight in my left eye. I was not healed that night and the people who prayed for me insisted that I was not healed because of my lack of faith.[4] They encouraged me to read the Bible more because, according to the apostle Paul, "faith cometh by hearing, and hearing by the word of God" (Romans 10:17 KJV). That seemed to be more of a chastisement than an encouragement for me on that night. The interplay of faith and the works of faith in the act of healing leave us with curious dilemmas. How much faith is enough in order to be healed? In my case, I believe the faith was there but God's plan was such that healing was not the better gift for my life.

Prayer and Healing

Prayer is also a key element in healing. In Mark 9:25-27, Jesus healed a demon-possessed young person after a failed attempt by his disciples. After the healing, the disciples inquired of Jesus in private, "Why could we not cast it out?" Jesus said to them, "This kind can come out only through prayer" (Mark 9:28-29). The implication is that the prayers of the disciples were not sufficient to accomplish the much-desired healing. Prayer unleashes the power of God on this earth, but fervent prayers of the righteous do not always accomplish the healing that we seek.

Joni Eareckson-Tada, a world-famous Christian advocate for people with disabilities, who lost the use of her arms and legs at the age of eighteen from a diving accident, recalls a healing service in which people of great faith prayed for her recovery. The healing did not come despite the faith and the prayers of the believers who gathered around her during this special service held specifically for her.[5] It is important for the church not to engage in faith and prayer conversations that have judgmental implications.

That said, it is true that God sometimes heals people in miraculous ways. We should always give God the glory for these signs and wonders of physical restoration. At a session of the Baltimore-Washington Annual Conference in May of 2012, a woman was suddenly healed of the blindness in her left eye. This was a cause for great rejoicing![6]

A pastor from the Eastern Pennsylvania Conference and his wife were told in their fifth month of pregnancy by two physicians that the mother's sonogram showed that their unborn child had no kidneys and would likely be stillborn or live for only a day or two. Over the course of a month, they had four more sonograms by three different doctors who all confirmed this report. The pastor and his wife were informed that kidneys grow in the first month, not in the last few months of pregnancy, and that there was no hope. The couple sought the prayers of God's people, and after two months of fervent prayer the fifth and sixth sonograms showed that kidneys had miraculously developed. This baby was born healthy and is thriving. The first doctor to see the new kidneys was totally amazed and said, "Other than a miracle, I have no explanation for this," while the second examining doctor said, "I have no explanation for this. All I can tell you is what was impossible is now possible." This miracle was an answer to prayer.[7]

Ministries of Healing

God heals through the skillful hands of physicians who bring life-giving surgeries and medications. A medical mission team, organized by the Central Congo Partnership of the Peninsula-Delaware Annual Conference, regularly visits the Democratic Republic of Congo to perform cataract surgeries on many who have little or no eyesight. The team comes home with stories of great joy as sight has been restored to many who had no hope of healing prior to this effort.[8]

I knew a United Methodist pastor who not only had two heart transplants but also a kidney transplant. The late Reverend LeRoy Schauer, a pastor in the Baltimore-Washington Conference, had a long and productive ministry as a result of these surgeries that extended his life. His witness to others facing similar surgeries not only brought encouragement but furthered awareness of the need for organ donors in this country through his testimony and "Organ and Tissue Donation Awareness Sundays."

We as a church have a ministry of healing that is a part of our faith. We experience the loving hand of God working supernaturally and through natural means to bring wholeness. But there are many ways that people can be healed that do not necessarily

> "Curing comes when we enter into life with Christ." S. Johnson

restore one's ability to walk, see, hear, or be relieved of pain, depression, anxiety, or cognitive disability. The apostle Paul spoke of the "thorn in the flesh" which he asked God three times to heal (2 Corinthians 12:8). His healing came through God's assurance that "My grace is sufficient for you, for power is made perfect in weakness" (2 Corinthians 12:9a). Instead of questioning God for not healing him, Paul proclaimed, "I will boast all the more gladly of my weaknesses, so that the power of Christ may dwell in me" (2 Corinthians 12:9b).

Father Cyril Axelrod is a Roman Catholic priest who was born deaf and gradually became blind from retinitis pigmentosa. The pairing of deafness and this form of blindness is a genetic condition known as Usher syndrome. Axelrod struggled mightily as he lost his eyesight because his vision was necessary to communicate through sign language. However, he testified to me that he thanked God for his blindness because it opened up to him a whole new world of ministry with persons who are both deaf and blind. He travels the world encouraging this community. Much of the strength of his witness comes from sharing the condition of being both deaf and blind.[9]

Experiencing Healing While Not Being Cured

Many people of faith who have not been physically restored to full function testify to the experience of healing as opposed to being cured. Rev. Jonathan Campbell, a pastor in the Greater New Jersey Annual Conference who has cerebral palsy, writes about his experience working as a chaplain in an institution for people with people with disabilities. One of the residents asked Campbell if he would pray for him to be healed. Campbell explained:

> I told Bob [not his real name] I would pray with him, but first I needed to tell him about how God healed me. Out of my mouth came my story of pain and fear. I told Bob how I hated myself and the world, and how God had worked in my life to help me understand that I did not need to be physically cured to be a whole person. God was healing me of the real problems in my life, the problems of hate, anger and fear. I told him about how I hoped God would use me to spread God's grace so more people could be healed from feeling like they have no value and no worth. Then I prayed for healing and wholeness in Bob's life.[10]

With that understanding it is essential to ask if a person with a disability wants prayer for healing. People with disabilities who find God's grace sufficient for their every need may find the offer offensive and patronizing. To insist on prayer for healing, even with positive intentions, brings a hurtful insinuation that without physical healing the person is not whole. We can also pray as Campbell did, that healing will come in ways that change one's perspective about one's disability. That is distinct from being physically cured. The body of Christ is inclusive of everyone as they are, including those with disabilities. Disability is one of the many forms of diversity that God has fashioned. We may never completely understand in this life why some people are healed and some are not, or why people have disabilities. We need to respect people as they are.

Beth Hopkins is a writer who has cerebral palsy. She objects to strangers approaching her with the intent of offering healing prayers because cerebral palsy is a part of who she is as a person. "To be healed of my disability is to change my physical state of being—which has been as it is since I was born—and this would mean completely redefining life as I know it. To not have a disability is to forego a large part of my identity. And I would hate to lose that on someone else's whim."[11]

We are assured from Scripture that no disability can separate us from the love of God in Christ Jesus (Romans 8:38-39) and that God works all things together "for good for those who love God, who are called according to [God's] purpose" (Romans 8:28).

Inclusion

The apostle Paul writes to the church in Corinth: "The members of the body that seem to be weaker are indispensable" (1 Corinthians 12:22). This is a profound, countercultural declaration of independence for the **disability community**! Chapter 12 in Paul's first letter to the Corinthians is a clarion call for the church to include everyone, especially those who some think are weaker. How amazing is this bias! Perhaps this insight came from Paul's own experience of disability. He uses the analogy of the human body to explain that no one is to be left out. "The eye cannot say to the hand 'I have no need of you.'" He also reminds body parts that they should not disqualify themselves for any reason. "If the foot would say, 'Because I am not a hand, I do not belong to the body,' that would not make it any less a part of the body" (1 Corinthians 12:15; also read verses 14-22).

Jennie Weiss Block writes in her book *Copious Hosting: A Theology of Access for People with Disabilities*:

> All who are serious about inclusion and allowing Christians with disabilities the opportunity to live out their true vocations need to learn about adaptive equipment, natural supports, and the various types of "high-tech" and "low-tech" assistive technology that are available to help people with disabilities increase, maintain, or improve functional capabilities and live and work independently. These accommodations have the potential to create incredible opportunities for people with disabilities within our church.[12]

Jesus showed sensitivity to the particular needs of a deaf man who was brought to him for healing. He modeled ways for us to provide **accommodations**. In Mark 7:31-37, Jesus pulled the deaf man aside from the crowd and communicated with the man in a visual way. He put his fingers in the man's ears, spat and touched his tongue, looked up to heaven, and sighed. This is visual communication tailored for the needs of this man so he would understand what was happening. Inclusion is simply that: adapting one's communication and behaviors and architecture in such a way that allows for equal access to what able-bodied people have.

An inclusive church asks, "Who is not at the table?" and strives to extend a hand of welcome in concrete ways to those who are missing. When I served an all-Deaf congregation in Baltimore, we asked who was not included. It did not take long to identify our exclusion of people who were physiologically deaf but did not use American Sign Language for communication. We realized we had **communication barriers** in place. A worship service rendered in the exquisite language of signs did not meet the needs of persons who were never exposed to sign language or who chose to function in the hearing world by speaking, **lip-reading**, and using **assistive listening devices**. The Deaf church members made the inclusive decision to install two kinds of listening systems, provide computerized assisted note-taking, and make available a printed copy of the sermon for these new attendees. When these accommodations were put in place, some talented new members joined the church. They gifted the congregation with a hard-of-hearing support group, help with hearing aids and listening devices, and workshops on issues related to seniors who become deaf later in life.

Later the Deaf church also noticed that people who were **deaf-blind** were not at the table. Persons who were deaf and blind could not see the signs, hear the voice interpreter, or benefit from the visual supports of the note-taker. They literally "felt the Word of the Lord" through tactile sign language rendered in the palm of the hand. Inclusion for this group meant providing someone to drive them to church, guide them around the building as needed and tactilely sign the worship service for them. Some used large print and **Braille** materials, which we were able to provide as well. When the deaf-blind community joined the church, one man became a part of the sign language choir. He brought to the church some of the most beautifully signed songs ever used in worship. A deaf-blind camp and a local chapter of the Association of the Deaf-Blind were established as an outgrowth of the ministry at the church. Inclusion and **integration** bring gifts that benefit the whole body.

There are many practical ways that congregations can model Paul's theology of inclusion of the entire body. More details about these kinds of accessibility options will be discussed later in this book.

A church that has an inclusive heart can meet the needs of people with any number of physical, cognitive, and emotional disabilities. The process starts with removing the barrier of negative attitudes. Often fear and ignorance prevent people from including those with disabilities in the circle of fellowship. When attitudinal barriers are removed people with disabilities are seen simply as people with potential and giftedness. Differences are viewed as part of the mosaic of life and not a cause for discomfort or rejection. In addition, when the attitudes have been healed, funds to procure the many accommodations needed are provided out of a sense of God's abundance.

Empowerment and Advocacy

The apostle Paul reminded the church of Corinth: "Those members of the body that we think less honorable we clothe with greater honor, and our less respectable members are treated with greater respect" (1 Corinthians 12:23). That is the meaning of *empowerment*. Being the voice for the voiceless and putting people with disabilities in the "driver's seat" of ministry is fundamental to the call of Christ for us to be the salt of the earth and the light of the world (Matthew 5:13-16). Advocacy was demonstrated when four men brought a man who was paralyzed to Jesus by removing the tiles from the roof (Mark 2:2-5). Advocacy happens any time the church is active in the world, speaking for social justice for people who are oppressed.

Jesus opened the scroll of Isaiah in his hometown of Nazareth and read, "The Spirit of the Lord is upon me, / because he has anointed me / to bring good news to the poor. / He has sent me to proclaim release to the captives / and recovery of sight to the blind, / to let the oppressed go free, / to proclaim the year of the Lord's favor" (Luke 4:18-19). Jesus' platform was social justice and he included people with disabilities in the mix. Jesus was sent specifically to those who experience marginalization and oppression.

Advocates are people who understand Jesus' teaching that people at the margin belong in the center. In inclusive churches, advocates find ways that empower people with disabilities to use their gifts and graces as full members of the body of Christ. **Self-advocacy** is the ultimate goal of inclusion so that people with disabilities speak for themselves, but this is greatly enhanced by the presence and power of able-bodied allies who assist by opening the door from within.

Advocacy with the disability community is a form of liberation theology. Gustavo Gutiérrez, a liberation theologian, explains it as a "theological reflection born of the experience of shared efforts to abolish the current unjust situation and to build a different society, freer and more human."[13] In fact, the field of **disability theology** is a branch of liberation theology.

Kyle Aiken Forder attends Los Altos United Methodist Church in the California-Pacific Annual Conference. Forder uses a wheelchair for mobility. The church is equipped architecturally for people who use wheelchairs and those with other forms of sensory and cognitive challenges. At this church they engage in advocacy that empowers. Forder is an assistant teacher of the middle school class. He has assisted with a sermon series, sung in the choir, and gone on a choir tour. His gifts are used effectively in the church, and both he and the church benefit from this kind of liberation ministry.[14]

The Americans with Disabilities Act (ADA) (1990)[15] is a federal law that requires businesses, banks, schools, and all government entities to provide accommodations for people with disabilities. This comprehensive law includes accessibility in the areas of transportation, communication, education, and employment. The law has radically changed life for the better for those in America with disabilities.

Religious institutions, however, are exempt from the ADA.[16] As a result the church often views such accommodations as an optional form of charity that they can bestow when they wish or if they have the money or desire to do so. According to Deborah Beth Creamer in her book *Disability and Christian Theology*:

> Rather than being a structure for empowerment, religious organizations have more often supported the societal structures and attitudes that have treated people with disabilities as objects of pity and paternalism. Relations between disability activists and religious groups became strained during the ADA lobbying process and have scarcely improved in subsequent years.[17]

The church needs to be out in the world advocating for the rights of people with disabilities. We can have an impact that liberates and empowers. Like the prophet Amos, who called the people of God to let "justice roll down like waters, and righteousness like an ever-flowing stream" (Amos 5:24), the church should be exposing the discrimination and marginalization of people with disabilities. The church can put a spotlight on this issue and call the world to stop abusing and ignoring people with disabilities and to create structures that enhance equality.

Scott Vickery, a United Methodist home missioner, worked as a special education teacher in a self-contained classroom for a number of years in Hattiesburg, Mississippi. His students had severe to profound cognitive and physical disabilities. An important part of his work as a teacher and as a Christian who is called to social justice ministry was to advocate for his students. He advocated for funding for specialized equipment and for opportunities for his students to take part in social events with typically developing peers. His advocacy also included helping parents learn how to speak up for their children with disabilities in order to access support services.[18]

Advocacy is the crown jewel of the disability trilogy of awareness, accessibility, and advocacy. Groups typically do not engage in advocacy and empowerment until awareness and accessibility have been achieved. This process takes time, patience, money, and the power of the Holy Spirit. But as true daughters and sons of John Wesley, the founder of the Methodist movement, we need to see ourselves as constantly "going on to perfection" in our walk with the Lord and in our ministries with the disability community.

Chapter 3
Labels and Etiquette

The old adage "sticks and stones may break my bones but words will never hurt me" is simply not true. The Book of James reminds us "how great a forest is set ablaze by a small fire! And the tongue is a fire" (James 3:5b-6a). When speaking to or about a person with a disability, the fire of prejudice, devaluation, and insensitivity can blaze hotter than any flame in a person's psyche. **Ableist** language is a product of **ableism**, which is a set of practices that promotes "discrimination or prejudice against individuals with disabilities."[1] Ableism creates stereotypes about the character and life situation of a person with disabilities such as assumptions of dependence, inferiority, infirmity, and weakness.

The term **handicap** has been erroneously thought of as describing people with disabilities begging on the street with a cap in their hand. But that is not the case. The word *handicap* dates back to the 1600s in England and referred to a bartering game in which the wager money was kept in a hat by the referee. Later the term was used in horse racing as an advantage given to an inferior horse by "handicapping" the more capable horse with weights. Not until 1915 did the word *handicap* first appear in an appeal as a description of a child with a disability.[2] The term *disability* is the preferred word in current use, rather than the older term *handicap*.

People-First Language

The use of **people-first language** in all conversations and written materials is an important way to show respect.[3] People-first language establishes the humanity of the person first and gives the description of the disability second. For example, it is better to say "the woman with a disability" rather than "the disabled woman." It is preferable to say "the man who has had his leg amputated" rather than "the amputee." There is much more to a person's life and character than his or her form of disability.

I knew a man who had a hearing loss since childhood and who felt like one big ear while growing up. There was so much emphasis on his hearing loss and his hearing aids that he did not feel like a regular child. When we lump people together with words like "the blind" or "the mentally ill," our language negates personhood.

There are more positive ways to describe disabilities. Speakers or writers should say "the man using a wheelchair for mobility" rather than "the man who is wheelchair bound" or "confined to a wheelchair." Use the terms "person with a cognitive challenge" or "someone who has an intellectual disability or developmental disability" instead of "mentally retarded." Labels such as "deaf and dumb," "deaf mute," "crippled," "crazy," "idiot," "invalid," "retard," or "moron" are offensive and should be avoided. A "handicapped" bathroom or parking space should be called an "accessible" bathroom or space.

Self-Identification

It is best to ask the person with a disability what description or label she or he would prefer. People have a variety of life experiences that can influence language and label choices. For example, people who have a hearing loss and use American Sign-Language (ASL) consider themselves members of the **Deaf community**.[4] They usually prefer that you refer to them as "Deaf" with a capital *D* because being Deaf is part of their cultural identity. Other people who have a hearing loss prefer to say they are "hearing impaired." The word *impaired* is offensive to the Deaf community because it refers to the loss of a function that they do not value. Deaf persons do not feel they are impaired in any way since ASL is quite adequate for their communication needs.

People with visual challenges sometimes wish to be called people who are "blind," while others prefer terms such as "low vision" or "visually impaired." Using "mental health condition or diagnosis" is far more respectful than saying that someone is "mentally ill" or "emotionally disturbed." A person who is "nonverbal" can better be described as one who "communicates with his or her eyes," or who "uses assistive devices."

The emphasis should be on what a person can do or what the device empowers a person to do. I knew a woman who used a wheelchair for mobility who spelled the word *disability* with a capital A in the middle—disAbility—to make that point clear. Some people like "differently abled" or "otherly abled" or "challenged," while others do not like those terms. Always seek the individual's preference and never assume that you know the proper terminology.

Biblical Imagery and Hymn Texts

Language is power, and we empower people with proper labels and positive language. It is a challenge for church leaders to begin to speak more in accessible, people-affirming ways. Some of the archaic language of our biblical texts and hymns can be offensive, reflecting a negative image of people with disabilities.

Psalm 58:4 describes the wicked "like the venom of a serpent, / like the deaf adder that stops its ear." Micah 7:16 proclaims, "The nations shall see and be ashamed / of all their might; / they shall lay their hands on their mouths; / their ears shall be deaf." This symbolism connects deafness with evil and disobedience.

We know that these are linguistic images and that the writers are not intentionally casting aspersions on deaf people, but such language harms in subtle ways. I used to teach deaf children after-school religious education classes at the Maryland School for the Deaf. Because of the preponderance of Bible stories about hearing people, many of the students believed that God was hearing and did not understand their signs. The only Bible stories about deaf people were those in which Jesus healed deaf people and turned them into hearing people.

When I served as the pastor in an all-Deaf church I would never choose a hymn like "This is my Father's world / and to my listening ears, / all nature sings and round me rings / the music of the spheres."[5] How might a Deaf person who attends a hearing church that provides a sign language interpreter feel about this song? For some the hearing-bias hymns are acceptable as these persons appreciate a variety of images in poetry even if they don't physically experience sound. Others feel excluded by this language. We should strive to choose language inclusive of ability and disability in our worship, just as we work to use language that is inclusive of gender and ethnicity. In that way we promote positive images for all.

In *The United Methodist Hymnal,* "O For a Thousand Tongues to Sing" stanza 6 has an asterisk that says "may be omitted."[6] This is in recognition that "hear him, ye deaf; his praise, ye dumb, your loosened tongues employ" is not in this day and age a helpful description of those with a hearing loss, nor does it describe their hope of heaven. Many feel that heaven is a place of equal access to communication, not necessarily a place where hearing is restored.

"Halo" Effect

One last word about language: I have made a case for positive, empowering language and imagery and for avoiding discriminatory labeling. There is one other type of language that can be equally destructive but cloaked in a veil of kindness. That language is characterized by what I call the **halo effect**. When a person with a disability is elevated to an overly positive position and praised excessively for being a "brave little soldier" or spoken of as more holy because of the "cross that they bear," this too is a form of abusive language.

Angela Orlando, a woman with a number of disabilities, describes it this way in her poem "Poster Child"[7]:

They point at me and say their lines
You are inspiring
You can do anything
You are a role model to everyone
We are so proud of you.

I die a little because I know the truth
I'm a fake
I do nothing to deserve such praise
There's no reason to admire me
My life is just a waste.

I begin to believe the propaganda
I can be more than this
I'll move on and never stop
I'll make my dreams come true
I'll show them what I can do

They tell me what they really think
It's a bad idea
You will fail
No, you can't do it
You are making trouble for all of us

I'm just a poster child
Smile!
You look so good on film

Your story is amazing
Keep up the good work

Just a poster child . . . and those who matter
don't believe in me.

We need to speak the truth in love at all times. When we are speaking respectfully, we won't be putting people down or elevating them to the larger-than-life Poster Child.

Etiquette

Aside from labels and language, there are a number of other important rules of **etiquette** to keep in mind when beginning ministry with people with disabilities. Some of the rules include:

1. Greet anyone you meet with a handshake, and use age-appropriate language. Speak directly to the person, not to a family member or interpreter. Assume the person can understand you.

2. Don't pretend you understand if you don't. State the part you have understood and try again, or ask a series of direct yes or no questions.

3. Repeat or rephrase your comments if the person doesn't seem to understand you.

4. When you realize that a person may not be hearing you, get their attention by lightly touching their arm. Make sure you are facing the person so she or he can read your lips. Keep your hands from covering your mouth, and have the lighting on your face, not behind you.

5. Enunciate but do not exaggerate your speech; speak clearly but do not shout.

6. If a person uses sign language and there is no interpreter, you may be able to communicate by writing back and forth.

7. If the person cannot see, state your name each time you meet, and be sure to say when you are leaving. Ask if the person wants you to describe what is happening around her or him, for instance, the food in a buffet line.

8. If someone is using a service or Guide Dog, remember that the animal is working and do not distract the animal by trying to pet the dog or talk to it.

9. To guide a person who is blind, offer to have the person clasp your bent elbow and walk slightly behind you. Provide verbal cues for turns and hazards.

10. Sit at eye level to speak with someone seated in a wheelchair or to a person of short stature.

11. Do not touch or move a person's wheelchair, crutches, cane, or other mobility device unless you are asked to do so. Many people consider their devices an extension of their bodies.

12. Offer assistance if someone may need it, but wait until the person accepts your help. Listen carefully and follow the person's instructions.

13. Don't worry about offending someone by saying things like "see you later," or "have you heard this?" People understand that these are not meant literally and probably use the terms themselves. Relax and be yourself![8,9]

The rules of etiquette that people with disabilities appreciate simply apply common sense and the awareness that people with disabilities are interested in the same things as people who do not have disabilities. People with disabilities are experts on themselves. They know what they like and do not like and what they can and cannot do. It always helps to have a sense of humor. Mistakes happen, but it is important to not take them too seriously. Stay positive and say you are sorry when you have gotten it wrong. People with disabilities are for the most part quite patient. Keep trying to communicate and never give up!

90% of deaf people have no one in the family to communicate effective.

Chapter 4
Deaf Culture

Deafness as a Culture and Not a Disability

I stood in the maternity ward a number of years ago with a family that had just given birth to a baby girl. Both parents were unable to hear and used American Sign Language (ASL) as their means of communication. I was there as their pastor to pray for and welcome the new member of the family. There was a sign language interpreter with them at the hospital in compliance with the Americans with Disabilities Act, a federal law that mandates communication access to people in public places and institutions.[1] The new parents were eagerly awaiting a visit from the doctor who would tell them the results of the hearing screening that is standard practice for newborn babies in most hospitals. The doctor arrived with a sad-looking face and through the interpreter let them know that the screening indicated a high probability that this child could not hear. Immediately both parents clapped, smiled, and hugged each other. The doctor wanted to know if the interpreter had gotten it right. He had just told them that their baby girl was deaf; he believed this was bad news and yet they were elated. The proud father, with eloquent signs, explained that since he and his wife were deaf this was indeed happy news for them. Deafness was their culture and way of life, not a disability. Sign language was their mode of communication. "I have my hands and my eyes. You have your ears and your mouth. We are different but equal," the new father explained.

This is the perspective of a person who is a part of the Deaf community or **Deaf culture**. When referring to this group it is expected that the *D* is capitalized.[2] According to a study at the Western Interstate Commission for Higher Education Mental Health Program:

Being unable to hear is only a part of being Deaf. In fact when the word is used in the cultural sense, hearing is one of the least important criteria used to delineate group membership. . . . [T]he culturally Deaf . . . define themselves by what they are instead of what they are not. They consider what they are as a positive trait, because it is tightly connected to their culture.[3]

During the years I served as pastor at Christ United Methodist Church of the Deaf, I learned that the use of American Sign Language was the hallmark of this lively community. ASL is a totally visual language with no speech, English grammar or syntax. It involves not only the hands but the head, eyes, and even nonverbal mouth movements. The church Deaf community included people of all ethnic backgrounds and socioeconomic strata, but to be a part of the culture a person had to be fluent in ASL.

Other cultural norms included the primacy of all forms of visual communication and the need to enhance this in as many ways as possible. Good lighting, the elimination of visual distractions and barriers, and the use of text pagers, video phones, flashing light alarm and alerting systems were all a part of it. In addition, the culture had a component of a supportive community that was warm and loyal. The members of the community were like a family and almost all personal business was community business. Faithfulness to each other and resourcefulness in times of discrimination empowered this community to often rise up and protest in one unified voice for the rights and the welfare of the community. I remember attending a mass transit hearing that was held in order to get community feedback as the city considered bus route changes. Many Deaf people came to protest the elimination of a bus line that was a vital means of transportation for a number of the church members.

Deaf Culture and "Hearing" Churches

Few hearing churches provide ASL access for people who are a part of the Deaf community. In the United States there are fewer than one hundred United Methodist churches providing ASL interpreting at their worship services.[4] This is due partly to the expense, the lack of knowledge about the community, and Deaf people's tendency to gravitate toward worship experiences that are exclusively for Deaf people. An all-Deaf worship experience would include an ASL-driven production of sermons, prayers, and songs at a reasonable speed, not at the speed that is required when there is a sign language interpreter keeping up with the spoken word. Leadership opportunities and culturally appropriate missions and Bible studies are also the norm at an all-Deaf church.

Some Deaf people have no interest in religious institutions for a variety of reasons. Some have not grown up with a religious background or have been turned off by negative experiences as a child. Others who don't have that much contact with the hearing world feel that church participation is largely for hearing people.

Sometimes a well-meaning church will provide a sign language interpreter and advertise such on their church's outdoor sign. Often they will be surprised that Deaf people have not come to take advantage of their efforts and expense. For many members of the Deaf community, breaking into an all-hearing social system where the only person they can have a reasonable conversation with is the hired sign language interpreter is far from desirable. Hearing people, who don't know ASL, no matter the amount of the heartfelt good will, typically face significant linguistic barriers when a Deaf person comes to the church. After a few words are exchanged in sign or scribbled on a piece of paper, the conversation ends and the hearing people slip away for lack of anything else to say.

Hospitality

However, there are many examples of successful ministries with the Deaf community in hearing churches. Churches that wish to embark on this ministry should pray and study the needs and the cultural norms of this unique culture. Here are some nonnegotiable signs of hospitality for people of the Deaf culture:

1. A quality ASL interpreter: The interpreter should not be a student or a family member but a paid, contracted professional who prepares adequately for the worship experience and for all parts of church life that the Deaf person wishes to join. Bible studies, potluck dinners, social activities, and mission trips all require language access, not just the worship service on Sunday morning.

2. Visual considerations: In whatever setting the Deaf person finds herself or himself, there need to be clear lines of vision. Adequate lighting, the elimination of background lights and shadows, and a distinct contrast between the color of the interpreter's clothing and hands are essential.

3. Visual alarms, alerts, and communications: The church should be wired for flashing light smoke alarms and doorbells. Church staff should be versed in how to receive and place video relay or **TTY** (a telephone device that incorporates a keyboard for typed messages)

phone calls. They should be aware that there may be a delay while the operator speaks and completes the connection. (The ADA law requires every state to provide communication technology.[5] To access a relay operator, people need only dial 711 and provide the phone number. Some Deaf people have their own phone number connected automatically to the relay system.

4. Socialization opportunities: Deaf people should be included in the social aspects of church, which will naturally lead to church members becoming familiar with American Sign Language. Sign language classes for hearing church members help build community as the language barriers come down.

5. Empowerment and service: A person who uses ASL can do more than sit in the front row and watch the interpreter. Members who are Deaf can read the Scripture, preach, teach a Bible class, or take part in congregational committees and mission projects.

Often a culturally Deaf family will attend a hearing church for the benefit of their hearing children. Ninety percent of all Deaf people who have children have hearing children, who are often referred to as **CODA**s, or children of deaf adults.[6] The church should be aware of the children's needs, allow them to flourish in the hearing world of the church, and not use them as interpreters.

Empowerment

Any church that reaches out to the Deaf community with sincerity, patience, a commitment for consistent provision of services, and empowerment will be blessed with the presence and giftedness of this amazing group of people. At the same time, denominations would do well to also support the stand-alone culturally Deaf churches as they minister with others who are better served there.

The Jacksonville United Methodist Deaf Faith Community Church in Jacksonville, Illinois (Illinois Great Rivers Conference), is one of these stand-alone culturally Deaf communities. Everyone here uses sign language and their pastor, until recently the Reverend Elke Sharma, is Deaf. As a Deaf faith community they focus on mission and ministries based on their unique interests and needs. Recently they began a new United Methodist Women's unit. Together, without any linguistic barriers since they all use ASL, they are planning outreach with youth at the Illinois School for the Deaf in Jacksonville, Deaf Camp, and the Hope School for the Deaf in Liberia, Africa. The group's motto is: "Because God and Jesus love us and we love others, we can listen and give with our hands and hearts in ministry to all!"[7]

Jacksonville, Illinois, is also the home of a United Methodist deaconess who is Deaf. Dr. Vae Rose Fultz reaches out to Deaf people who have developmental challenges and are residents of neighborhood group homes. I visited her and saw how she brings enrichment programs and spiritual nurture to these residents through her ability to communicate in ASL. Fultz's many years of working at the Illinois School for the Deaf has helped to sensitize her to this population that is often overlooked after graduation from high school.

The church is as yet to fully experience the gifts that members of the Deaf community can bring to the whole body of Christ. The fields are ripe for harvest as we reach out and empower.

Chapter 5
Hard of Hearing and Late-Deafened

Deaf Culture vs. the Experience of People Who Are Hard of Hearing and/or Late-Deafened

I have divided the conversation about hearing loss into two chapters intentionally because the American Sign Language (ASL)-using Deaf community and people who are hard of hearing and **late-deafened** have huge linguistic and cultural differences. Despite assumptions by hearing people that those who have a hearing loss have much in common, many fundamental issues divide these communities.

Nancy Kingsley, a woman who has became progressively hard of hearing throughout her lifetime, explains it this way:

> Culturally Deaf people belong to the Deaf community while hard of hearing and late-deafened people belong to the hearing community. Culturally Deaf people use American Sign Language; hard of hearing and late-deafened people use spoken language or Signed English. Culturally Deaf people do not consider deafness to be a disability. Hard of hearing and late-deafened people find that deafness brings relationship and career difficulties.[1]

Both groups share the experience of living with a hearing loss but each uses a different way to communicate. The degree of deafness is not the deciding factor in choosing to belong to the signing Deaf community or to the **hearing community**. I have known people who are totally deaf who did not learn sign language and choose to speak and lip-read. I have also met people who are hard of hearing with enough residual hearing to use a telephone who identify with the Deaf community in their preference for ASL and Deaf culture. It is a matter of individual choice, influenced by family systems, onset of deafness, educational opportunities, and personal communication factors. The church needs to be respectful of the spectrum of needs and choices and never decide for persons what language or equipment they should use to assist them in worship and fellowship.

Many people who are hard of hearing or late-deafened have had or continue to have some hearing capabilities. They seek ways to enhance their residual hearing through the use of hearing aids and assistive technology. Some choose to have a surgical procedure known as a **cochlear implant**, which functions like an artificial organ of hearing. A cochlear implant is used with a processor that allows a person to hear sound; with therapy users can discern sounds and words, some with more success than others.

In addition, persons who are hard of hearing or late-deafened often use lip-reading skills and seek written English text for clarity.[2] The general rule is that no more than 35 percent of what is spoken can be accurately lip-read so the art of lip-reading has much to do with context, filling in the gaps, and attending to other visual cues.[3]

Remaining part of the hearing world, hard of hearing and **late-deafened** persons prefer to use their native spoken tongue. People who become deaf or hard of hearing later in life don't usually learn sign language.[4] They may think they need to learn to sign, but that would only be successful if everyone in their life also learned to sign so they would have people with whom they could communicate. But if they do sign, they usually do so to support their understanding of spoken English through the use of signed English. This is distinct from ASL in that it uses English grammar word-order.

Implications for the Church

The number of people who are hard of hearing or late-deafened far outranks the Deaf community. According to the National Institute on Deafness and Other Communication Disorders, there are approximately 36 million Americans with some degree of hearing loss, the vast majority of whom do not use ASL.[5] This has implications for the church. Far more people would benefit from assistive listening devices and visual access to English than need an ASL interpreter. Churches need to understand that if they are offering sign language classes it is rarely a communication solution for persons who are losing their hearing. ASL fluency requires years of practice, and failure to learn can be one more disappointment in the journey of isolation that hearing loss often brings.

Theologian William Barclay experienced hearing loss and once prayed:

> O God, the trouble about being deaf is that most people find deaf folks just a nuisance. They sympathize with people who are blind and lame; but they just get irritated and annoyed with people who are deaf. And the result of this is that deaf people are apt to avoid company, and so get more and more lonely, and more and more shut in. . . . Give me the perseverance not to let this trouble get me down, and not to let it cut me off from others. And help me to remember that whatever happens, there is nothing can stop me from hearing your voice.[6]

The hard of hearing or late-deafened community has some of its largest numbers among senior citizens. The National Institute on Deafness and Other Communication Disorders notes a strong relationship between aging and hearing loss: 18 percent of adults forty-five through sixty-four years old have a hearing loss, 30 percent of adults between the ages of sixty-five and seventy-four, and 47 percent of adults seventy-five years old or older have a hearing loss.[7] According to the "2010 State of the Church: Congregation Life Survey," the median age of a United Methodist member in the United States today is fifty-seven. Thirty-seven percent of North American United Methodists are between the ages of forty-five and sixty-four, 34 percent are between the ages of sixty-five and eighty-four, and 5 percent are eighty-five and older.[8] That means that many of our members may have a hearing loss and more will acquire one.

It is likely that many of our church members with hearing loss are in denial about this and miss much of what is being said in church. Many, like Barclay, are grieving and may withdraw as they perceive that the world around them treats them as a nuisance.

Rev. Nancy Hale, a United Methodist elder in the New York Annual Conference, shares about her experience of losing her hearing.

> I think denial is part and parcel of any experience with disability, but in the case of hearing loss, it is easier to pretend that you don't have a disability. Hearing loss is an invisible disabling condition; there's no wheelchair or cane or limp to give you away. In fact, if you are skilled enough in pretending, you can coast right along, fooling people into believing that you don't have any kind of disablement. The inescapable truth, however, is that pretending and living in denial only get you so far, and can cause a lot of grief along the way.[9]

Hospitality

A ministry with people who are losing their hearing or are deaf but do not use ASL must be based on the understanding that each person has a unique set of needs for communication. Ministry involves first and foremost a spirit of genuine hospitality. Hospitality is more than offering a coffee cup and pen with the church's name on it. True hospitality listens to the person with the intent of truly communicating, listening and speaking in ways that are as barrier free as possible.

Some important communication tips from the Hearing Loss Association of America include the following advice regarding speaking to a person with a hearing loss:

1. Face the person directly.

2. Avoid noisy environments.

3. Be sure you are not standing in front of a light source that obscures your face.

4. Get the person's attention before you begin to speak.

5. Ask how you can facilitate communication. You may need to use a pencil and paper.

6. Don't shout but speak clearly at a moderate pace.

7. Don't hide your mouth, eat, or chew gum while talking.

8. Rephrase your statement if you are not understood.

9. Use facial expressions and gestures.

10. Give clues when changing subjects or simply say "new subject."

11. Be patient, show respect, and maintain a sense of humor with a positive and relaxed attitude.[10]

In terms of communication accessibility during worship services and church events, strive to do some or all of the following:

1. Everything should be as visual as possible. Printed copies of the sermon, along with projected printed announcements, hymns, and Scriptures are vitally important.

2. The kind of assistive listening devices (FM, Infrared, or loop) that the church purchases should be tested by the members who need them to hear. There are many variables and each system has its advantages.

3. Churches can provide communication access real-time translation (**CART**) **captioning**, C-Print (a speech-to-text system), or computer assisted note-taking to further document and project in printed English what is being spoken in worship. All videos and other media used in the service or other church functions need to be captioned.

4. Some people benefit from the services of an oral interpreter. This is a person who mouths the words that are being spoken, placing a second set of lips closer to the person, and making it easier to lip-read and understand.

5. A support group for people with hearing loss can be a wonderful way to build Christian community and share what is working in the way of communication aids.

Empowerment

The possibilities are endless and so are the opportunities for people with hearing loss to be in ministry and leadership in the church.

Dr. Thomas Hudspeth is one of many United Methodist pastors with a hearing loss. He serves at Lovers Lane United Methodist Church in the North Texas Annual Conference. He was born hard of hearing, uses hearing aids, and was mainstreamed into hearing schools. Hudspeth later experienced the world of signing and the Deaf community. He walks in both worlds now, ministering to all of the language needs of the community. Hudspeth says, "God doesn't call half of you . . . God calls ALL of you."[11]

And so it is that God is about the business of using gifted laypersons and clergy with hearing loss for all kinds of ministry. The language of the soul communicates loudly and clearly.

Chapter 6
Vision Loss

Tale of Two People

Recently I met an old friend who I had not seen in a long time. In the past my friend had a successful career in advertising. I was shocked to learn that in the years since we last encountered each other, my friend had become almost totally blind from glaucoma and was having great personal difficulty with the adjustment. My friend explained to me that everything possible had been tried but eventually there would be complete loss of vision. I could feel the pain and sadness.

When I served Christ UMC of the Deaf in Baltimore, there was a hearing member named Mary Smith who was totally blind. The Deaf church had a history of moving from church to church because they did not own a church building. At one time the annual conference trustees decided to move them to a church in east Baltimore that had recently closed. Mary and a few other hearing people had been members of the now-closed congregation. Since they had always gone to that church, they continued to attend even though the service was conducted in American Sign Language and most of the attendees were Deaf. The obvious issue was that Mary could not see the signs and the Deaf people could not hear her voice. Communication was less than ideal but the impact she had on the congregation was significant. Born totally blind, Mary was never deterred by this challenge. She went to the Maryland School for the Blind where she learned Braille along with **orientation and mobility skills**. She was able to go to college. She was then hired by her alma mater to be a teacher's aide and worked for the school from then on. Mary lived in her own house, raised her children, arranged for her own transportation, and took vacations with family and friends. Worship was important to her and she could walk to the church from her house. She told me she came to "help the deaf understand the meaning of independence."

Initially the Deaf church members were uneasy around her but she learned a little sign language and could feel their signs in her hands. She would often volunteer to sing for the church service, her lyrics signed by the interpreter. The Deaf people would be ministered to, not by her voice, but by the strength of her personality standing before them in worship of God.

Blindness or partial loss of vision can bring pain as well as victories in overcoming challenges.

Facts and Figures

Vision loss affects many people. Statistics vary, and indicate that between 14 and 21 million adults in the United States have a significant loss of vision.[1] According to one survey there are approximately 60,000 legally blind children in the United States.[2] Globally there are approximately 185 million people with partial or complete vision loss, with the rate nearly four times higher in the developing world.[3]

Everyone with vision loss has a unique story, as the causes for vision loss are many. Some of the more common causes of vision loss are cataracts, macular degeneration, glaucoma, diabetic retinopathy, retinitis pigmentosa, eye injuries, and retinopathy of prematurity. In addition there are preventable vision losses found in developing countries. These conditions such as trachoma, river blindness, and vitamin A deficiency can be prevented with education, improvements in diet and hygiene, and access to medical care. More than 90 percent of the world's blind people live in developing countries.[4]

Other eye conditions can be corrected with eyeglasses or contact lenses. These include nearsightedness; farsightedness; presbyopia, which causes difficulty focusing and is more common in older adults; and astigmatism, in which vision is distorted due to the cornea shape. Many people wear eyeglasses as a result of these common conditions.[5]

Hospitality

Given the complex physiology of blindness and the variations due to age of onset, educational opportunities, and socioeconomic considerations, the church needs to accommodate people on an individual basis. There are many ways that churches can be accessible to people with vision loss. These include the following:

1. Assistance with transportation for worship and events during the week.

2. Guiding around the building with verbal cues as to what is ahead, such as steps, curves, and doorways.

3. Giving a verbal overview of the order of worship or event.

4. Braille or large-print materials (bulletins, hymnals, Bible study materials).

5. Providing digital copies of materials for use with screen readers.

6. Audio description of things that are happening in the service that can be seen but not heard.

7. Use of audiotaped study materials and volunteer readers.

8. Priority seating.

9. Signage with Braille and large raised letters.

10. Improved lighting in the sanctuary, classrooms, and hallways.

11. Contrasting colors at the leading edges of steps.

12. Tactile or **cane-detectable** warnings of hazards.[6]

The increasingly wonderful world of technology has expanded the opportunities for access even more with talking computers, refreshable Braille computer displays, and software to enlarge images on the screen. Contrasting letter and background colors can also be programmed on computers for people who can see one color better than another. Magnification devices such as a close-captioned television (**CCTV magnifier**) enlarge printed text, photos, or even the letters on a medicine bottle or the numbers on paper money.

Wilhelmina Young is an active lay member of the Eastern Pennsylvania Conference of The UMC who has a vision loss. She attends annual conference and is aided by the use of a CCTV magnifier. When documents are distributed during the conference she slips them under the CCTV magnifier display and follows along as the letters on the paper are magnified on the screen in front of her.

In addition, some people with vision loss choose to have the assistance of a Guide Dog. Dogs should be welcome in church just as any other guide would be welcomed. People should not pat or interact with a Guide Dog while the dog is working. If the dog is distracted it may not be as attentive to the needs of the person, which can pose a safety hazard.[7]

Empowerment

Accessibility always leads to empowerment. People with vision loss have as many ways to serve as Christians who have intact vision. In The United Methodist Church we currently have a number of elders and deacons who have vision challenges. Rev. Nancy Webb, Rev. Kathy Reeves, Rev. Dr. Eric Pridmore, Rev. Mitch Galloway, and Rev. Dr. Robert Walker are some of our many United Methodist pastors who have served effectively with vision loss. Laypeople who are blind or have low vision can serve as lay readers, ushers, greeters, teachers, choir members, and organists, just to name a few areas of ministry.

Elizabeth Memorial United Methodist Church in Charleston, West Virginia, has a gifted, trained musician who is legally blind. Natasha Rashwan sings in the choir and the praise band on a regular basis, sometimes performing solos. According to her pastor, Rev. Frank Shomo, she is an asset to the worship service. For the members at Elizabeth Memorial, Natasha is not a musician who is blind. She is a member of the body of Christ, using her God-given talent for the edification of all.

The world has yet to see what members of the blind community can do when they are fully empowered in ministry. Rashwan commented that "God uses people who are different to get his point across. I am blessed to be used by God to bring a different point of view."[8]

Chapter 7
Mobility Challenges

Firsthand Experience with Mobility Challenges

A number of years ago I traveled with the Deaf choir on a concert tour with a woman who used a wheelchair for mobility. She had a wheelchair-accessible van and a motorized scooter, so I assumed those accommodations would be all that was needed to ensure easy access. I was in for the learning experience of my life. The weeklong tour became an immersion in what it is like to use a wheelchair in a world that is far from accessible. The first thing I discovered was that accessible parking was often being used by people who did not have accessible parking permits or tags. Also, people would often park so close to the van that it would be impossible to have enough room to raise and lower the van's hydraulic lift. I noticed for the first time how many curbs were not cut, how many doorways had sills too high for a wheelchair to pass through, how many doors were not wide enough, how many accessible bathroom stalls were too small to turn around in, and how many light switches, sinks, and paper towel dispensers were too high to reach.

I also discovered that the equipment supposedly available to assist people in wheelchairs is not always functioning or available. The choir member who used a wheelchair entered the front door of the church where we were to perform our most important concert of the week. I was told there was a lift that she could use to be brought up to the sanctuary level, only to discover that the key for the lift was nowhere to be found. They had not used the lift in a long time and were not sure where to find the custodian. I recall running around the facility frantically searching for the key because there was no other way for her to be a part of the choir. When the key was finally found, no one knew how to work the lift, but my friend figured it out on her own.

I heard people ask the woman who used the wheelchair rude questions about her "condition." Others would not talk to her directly by sitting at eye level but would instead ask me to tell her things. I also learned another very important fact: life as a wheelchair-user is expensive. Much of the specialized equipment she had was costly and insurance did not cover most of what she needed. She lived on the edge of poverty in order to pay for purchasing and maintaining the equipment that was necessary for her to function independently. I was never the same after that "wheelchair week." There is so much more that our churches can do to enable participation as we intentionally pursue ministry with people who use wheelchairs and other aids for mobility.

Facts and Figures

Mobility challenges are many and they come with age, disease, accidents, birth trauma, congenital issues, war, amputation, and so on. Strokes and arthritis are the two most common reasons that people use mobility devices. Multiple sclerosis, amputations, and spinal cord injuries frequently lead to the need for wheelchair use.[1] The natural progression of aging also brings decreasing strength and an increased chance of injuries that affect mobility.[2]

According to recent statistics there are more than three million wheelchair users in the United States and over ten million people who use other walking aids.[3] Of course, not everyone with decreased mobility uses a device. Some people find it hard to stand for any length of time, walk distances, rise from a low surface, or balance. In addition there are people whose mobility challenge is related to difficulty moving or controlling their arms, their hands, or their neck.

31

Hospitality

The most recognized symbol of the disability movement is the universal logo showing a stylized person seated in a wheelchair printed in white on a blue background. In fact, when the word *accessibility* comes to mind most people immediately think of a wheelchair ramp. A ramp is a good start, but having a ramp and no other kinds of accessibility is arguably worse than having nothing at all. And some ramps, if not constructed at the proper incline and width are actually dangerous to use. One person commented, "It's ten times easier for me to buy a pizza or beer than to get into my synagogue."[4]

Faith communities can do much to provide access. Morningside United Methodist Church (UMC) in Salem, Oregon, has done a good bit of work in order to make their building accessible. They have made **pew cut**s by shortening two pews in the sanctuary for wheelchair seating, installed an accessible photocopier that has an adjustable control panel, turned a restroom into an accessible unisex family restroom, and are installing automatic door openers. Their sanctuary chancel rises nearly twenty inches above the sanctuary floor level and they are considering installing a **platform lift**. They have a lower coat-rack rod that is an accessible place for hanging coats. Doorknobs have all been replaced with lever handles. The trustees, in dialogue with the Disabilities Connections Committee at Morningside UMC, believe in addressing needs promptly. They work with other church committees to make the church as accessible as possible and ask for suggestions from church members.[5]

Signage is another consideration when providing mobility accessibility. When getting around is a challenge, having clearly marked signs showing where to find the accessible entrance, sanctuary, and accessible restrooms can save a lot of unnecessary steps and fatigue. Adding accessibility information to the church website can help people with disabilities plan their visit in advance.

Bathrooms are particularly important. I visited a church recently and was met at the door by a young man who uses a wheelchair for mobility. The first thing he said was, "Make my pastor fix the bathroom for me." Apparently the bathroom was not big enough to accommodate his wheelchair. When he had to use the restroom, someone had to assist him and this was embarrassing to him. Many people with mobility challenges do not attend church because of inaccessible bathrooms. As some say, "If we can't go, we won't come!"[6]

Other important accessibility considerations include:

1. Accessible parking spaces with adjacent unloading space.

2. Curb cuts that are kept free of debris and snow.

3. Street level or ramped entrances, with the ramps no steeper than one foot of length for every one inch of rise.

4. Doorways at least thirty-two inches wide with a level platform outside the door.

5. Elevators with lower control panels, tactile buttons and signs, and voice announcements.

6. Ramp and stair handrails that extend twelve inches beyond the top and bottom.

7. Firm, low-pile, unpadded carpeting or floor surfaces with reduced slickness.

8. Accessible source of water, such as paper cups next to the water fountain.

9. Bathrooms with grab bars next to the toilet, higher toilet seats, and a way to close the door.

10. Sinks at the appropriate levels with knee clearance under the sink and lever-type faucets.

11. Towel and soap dispensers within reach (no higher than forty-eight inches) and mirrors positioned so a seated person can see herself or himself.[7]

Transportation is also a need for many with mobility challenges. Rose City Park United Methodist Church in Portland, Oregon, partners with a local agency called "Ride Connection" to offer weekly rides to church, using a van owned by an organization that doesn't need it on Sundays.[8] Along with a ride there is often the need for an "accessibility buddy" who assists the person using the wheelchair in maneuvering around in the church.

It is understandable that many churches do not have the means to make immediate drastic architectural changes. Some church buildings are historic landmarks, which require additional considerations. Elevators are indeed costly. However, there is always something that can be done, grants to apply for, and memorial money that can be designated to this life-giving work of accessibility. An annual audit can become a long-range game plan for how the church can become more and more accessible as funds are gathered.

Empowerment

Further, *The Book of Discipline of The United Methodist Church, 2012* mandates that when building a new church or when cost of the remodeling of a church or parsonage "will exceed 25 percent of the value of the existing structure or require mortgage financing, then the local church shall first . . . analyze the needs of the church and community . . . and develop an accessibility plan including chancel areas."[9] An accessible chancel sends a strong message that a person with a mobility challenge is as equally valued and needed in worship leadership as an able-bodied person.

Disability ministry is about making a way for the gifts and graces of all. The body of Christ will not be complete without the inclusion of the people with mobility challenges. Accessibility is always a work in progress, but as we carry out each step we will find sufficient grace to meet every challenge.

Chapter 8

Cognitive/Intellectual/ Developmental Disabilities

Dr. Henri Nouwen's Journey

Dr. Henri J. M. Nouwen, a theologian, seminary professor, and author, spent a number of years working at L'Arche Daybreak Community in Toronto, Canada. L'Arche is an international federation of communities, based on the Beatitudes,[1] which was founded by Jean Vanier in 1964 in Canada. Each L'Arche community consists of one or more homes in ordinary neighborhoods where people with disabilities and their helpers live together in shared households. According to their charter, L'Arche homes give people with intellectual disabilities a place to be valued and to grow into their potential. The homes exemplify the unity of the body of Christ and serve as a sign to the world of true Christian hospitality and integration.[2] Nouwen writes about Adam, the core member that he worked with on a daily basis:

> Adam did not have unique heroic virtues: he did not excel in anything that newspapers write about. But I am convinced that Adam was chosen to witness to God's love through his brokenness. To say this is not to romanticize him or to be sentimental. Adam was, like all of us, a limited person, more limited than most, and unable to express himself in words. But he was also a whole person and a blessed man. In his weakness he became a unique instrument of God's grace. He became a revelation of Christ among us.[3]

Facts and Figures

The world of cognitive, intellectual, and developmental disabilities is broad and complex. One to 3 percent of the population is diagnosed with an intellectual or developmental disability within the first seventeen years of life. These may include Down syndrome, autism, and cerebral palsy, which may or may not include cognitive challenges. Other cognitive disabilities are acquired later, due to traumatic brain injuries, degenerative diseases, brain tumors, or cognitive changes due to psychiatric conditions. Dementias, including Alzheimer's disease and cognitive changes brought on by strokes, are also considered cognitive disabilities. Learning disabilities such as dyslexia, attention deficit hyperactivity disorder, and sensory processing disorder come under the umbrella of cognitive disabilities. Persons with intellectual disabilities may have difficulty with attending to and processing information. While learning is possible, it may happen at a slower pace. Minor learning challenges may remain **hidden disabilities**, while people with more profound needs will often need lifelong support and assistance.[4]

According to the American Association on Intellectual and Developmental Disabilities (AAIDD), "our understanding of the causes of intellectual disability focuses on the types of risk factors (biomedical, social, behavioral, and educational) and the timing of exposure (prenatal, perinatal, and postnatal) to those factors."[5] The AAIDD considers intellectual disability to be a condition that affects both cognitive skills and adaptive behavior. Rather than being an unchangeable diagnosis, the condition can be improved by appropriate supports and services. The goal of the AAIDD is to improve the functioning and self-esteem of people with intellectual disabilities so they can have fulfilling lives.[6]

Hospitality

The church can be a vital force in the lives of people with intellectual, cognitive, and developmental disabilities; and the presence and gifts of this same community are just as important in order for the body of Christ to be complete. Dr. Erik W. Carter, author of *Including People with Disabilities in Faith Communities: A Guide for Service Providers, Families & Congregations,* noted, "The potential for congregations to dispense grace, extend relationships, and affect the lives of people with developmental disabilities and their families is enormous, but these rich and deep reservoirs of support remain largely untapped."[7]

According to Carter there are a number of ways that churches can be particularly helpful to community members with cognitive disabilities:

1. Building friendships and natural social connections.

2. Planning recreational and leisure activities in order to have fun together.

3. Linking people with vocational and skill-development opportunities.

4. Providing transportation to worship and other faith community activities.

5. Offering opportunities for service and volunteer work.

6. Supporting expanded housing options and choices.

7. Providing inclusive, age-appropriate faith development and religious education.

8. Supporting participation through matching people with "buddies" and helpers.[8]

In each case the service should match the needs and desires of the individual and be accompanied with a good bit of pre-thought and training for those providing the supports. Furthermore, people with intellectual and cognitive challenges are often tied into a number of government and educational resources. As congregations partner with formal agencies, they can often fill in the service gaps for mutually beneficial collaboration.

A nonprofit organization that provides supportive living programs for adults with developmental disabilities and traumatic brain injuries regularly brings interested participants to the Paoli UMC in southeastern Pennsylvania for worship, socialization, and fellowship meals. The partnership of church and a state-supported agency enhances the quality of life for the adults in these group homes. A number of the church members extend friendship and hospitality to the attendees.

Advocacy

Churches can also be out in the world providing hope and advocacy for people with developmental, cognitive, and intellectual challenges.

James (not his real name) was a young adult who was deaf and blind that I knew a number of years ago. He lived in a group home for cognitively and physically challenged young people. The care at this particular nonprofit group home was substandard. The staff routinely helped themselves to his clothing and personal belongings. His health club membership was used by the staff for their personal pleasure, while James was left at home in his room for hours. According to James it was not unusual for the staff to put ear drops in his eyes and eye drops in his ears and no amount of protest changed the situation. The Deaf church became aware of this while he was attending the church-sponsored deaf-blind camp. A mighty wave of protest came crashing in on this nonprofit agency the week after camp ended and changes began happening. James ultimately decided he wanted to live with a family and again the church got involved and helped him achieve his goal. Congregations can act when there is injustice.

The vast majority of group homes provide good care and support for their clients but government funding is often inadequate, leaving these programs struggling to pay for staff salaries, home repairs, and programming. The church can advocate on behalf of these institutions by insisting that state and local legislators keep these programs in their budgets. Without protests from social justice advocates, government agencies cut programs affecting vulnerable populations during tight economic times.

Cunningham Children's Home in Urbana, Illinois, is a project supported by the United Methodist Women of the Illinois Great Rivers Annual Conference. This is a home for children and youth who have a number of cognitive and emotional needs. Each year Cunningham sponsors a Mission Day that provides confirmation students and youth from around the conference a chance to meet the children and youth of the home and to build relationships. This kind of friendship is vitally important for everyone involved as it builds bridges of understanding and hope.[9]

United Methodist Women support the Rosa Valdez Early Childhood Learning Center in West Tampa, Florida. This preschool program serves seventy children from inner-city families, some of whom have disabilities. As an example of the services provided, the program supports a seventy-year-old woman who cares for her adult son, who is profoundly disabled. The woman's teen-aged daughter and her three-year old son (who has autism and behavior challenges), also live with her. "Rosa" as the center is called, helped the three-year-old learn ways of communicating without getting angry and to play without hurting others. This program freed up the family so that they could go to work and school knowing that the child was in good hands.[10]

Another important ministry that the church can offer is that of **respite** and support for families with loved ones with developmental disabilities. Families have round-the-clock responsibilities and find themselves exhausted and alone as they navigate through daily life routines as well as advocate for educational and government assistance. There is much that the supportive community of a congregation can do. More ideas will be discussed later in this book.

Congregations, conferences, and United Methodist Women organizations need to carefully examine what kinds of services they are willing and able to provide. Not every church is able to meet every need. Furthermore, churches should not be put in a position to compromise their core missional goals because of issues of separation of church and state that could arise as they work with government-supported programs. And in all things, persons with disabilities need to be involved in the decision making around the activities and services in which they wish to participate.[11]

Safe Sanctuaries

Churches must take care to include intellectually challenged people in their "Safe Sanctuary" policies. According to Joy Thornburg Melton, author of *Safe Sanctuaries: The Church Responds to Abuse, Neglect, and Exploitation of Older Adults,* screening and selection procedures for staff and volunteers need to include applications, interviews, personal references, and criminal background checks. Safe Sanctuaries operation policies and procedures should address issues such as having an adequate number of volunteers and staff in each ministry, providing first aid training, and having an open door policy.[12]

All United Methodist churches are required to have background checks and protocols that ensure safety for children, youth, and **vulnerable adults** within the ministry settings of the church. This includes architectural concerns such as having windows in every classroom door so that people can see into each room at all times. Rules need to be in place mandating that two nonrelated adults are to be present at all times when working with young people or vulnerable adults. Drop off and pick up procedures for church school and youth activities are also crucial. Having these procedures in place is especially important when dealing with people with intellectual disabilities.[13]

Empowerment

The gifts and graces of people with intellectual disabilities should be highlighted in every church. There are numerous tasks that members with cognitive differences can do successfully in service to God and the church. There is a place in the choir, in skits and plays, as ushers, on the acolyte committee, in the office, or in the building and grounds maintenance department where people with intellectual challenges can bless the congregation and experience the joy of service. University UMC in San Antonio, Texas, hosts such a ministry. Day program participants set up and take down tables and chairs, shred paper, serve food and clean up after a senior meal program, and prepare materials for church school classes.[14]

Every year the Roswell UMC near Atlanta, Georgia, holds a Christmas pageant, performed by members of the Noah's Ark Class for intellectually challenged adults. The participants see the performance as a way of giving back to their church and being in ministry along with everyone else. The sanctuary is always packed for the pageant through which the story of Christ's birth is told in wonderful new ways through the incarnational presence on the stage of the class members.[15] Imagine if every faith community would offer this kind of ministry! What a rich and blessed church we would have!

Chapter 9
Mental Health

Family Story

My grandmother suffered with a bipolar disorder. As a child I did not understand what this meant, but I observed a number of strange behaviors and overheard my parents talking about her. She had periods of high energy during which she would make many lemon meringue pies, go shopping, and charge thousands of dollars. She would also have times of depression where she did not even have the energy to get out of her overstuffed living room chair. My mother told me later that several times grandmother had been treated at a mental health facility; she even had been given shock treatments for depression. All of this was shrouded in an air of secrecy and shame. I learned early that her illness was not something that one should talk about to friends or neighbors and that there were strange dynamics between Grandmother and her children. Sometimes her adult children took over the executive functions of her life in ways that almost made them her parent.

However, Grandmother was a bright, witty, and musically talented woman. She never had any formal music lessons but she could play quite well "by ear" on her old mahogany upright piano in the living room. She was born in 1885 and lived in a time when there was much less understanding of mental health issues and fewer treatment options. Her family of origin no doubt contributed to her difficulties. Her father was an alcoholic who used to beat the children with a buggy whip when he was drunk. Grandmother and her seven siblings lived in poverty. She went to school until the age of eight and was then sent to work in a clothing mill. She was paid thirty cents a day for working long shifts.

Grandmother married young. She and my grandfather moved to the city and had five children in close succession. When she was in her forties and having episodes of depression, her doctor told her to have more children to get her "mind off of her problems." Following this questionable advice she plunged into even deeper depression. She attempted to abort her last child—my father—but was unsuccessful. She told my mother that she also considered committing suicide by jumping into a lake in the middle of the winter but changed her mind at the last minute. Of course, I would not be writing this account if she had succeeded. As a result of knowing my grandmother, I am forever touched by the sadness, **stigma**, and misunderstanding that people with mental illness face. I am sure most families have a story or two like this if they are willing to admit it. Mental health struggles are a part of being human, but the stigma is great. This is just one tiny account out of millions of people through the ages and around the world who live with a variety of mental health conditions.

Facts and Figures

According to the National Alliance on Mental Illness (NAMI), a mental health issue is a

> medical condition that disrupts a person's thinking, feeling, mood, ability to relate to others and daily functions. Just as diabetes is a disorder of the pancreas, mental illnesses are medical conditions that often result in a diminished capacity for coping with the ordinary demands of life. Serious mental illnesses include major depression, schizophrenia, bipolar disorder, obsessive compulsive disorder (OCD), panic disorder, posttraumatic stress disorder (PTSD) and borderline personality disorder.[1]

Approximately 61.5 million Americans experience a mental health disorder in a given year. One in seventeen persons lives with a serious mental illness.[2]

Mental Health Misconceptions

Mental illness is mentioned in the Bible. We read about King Saul who suffered with episodes of "[raving] within his house" (1 Samuel 18:10). Young David was called in to play his harp in order to bring relief (16:23). We know the story of the Gerasene man who was filled with legions of unclean spirits that caused him to hurt himself and to have unusual strength that enabled him to break any chains that were to subdue him (Mark 5:1-20). In the Book of Acts, Governor Festus accused Paul of having mental illness: "Too much learning is driving you insane!" (Acts 26:24). When Peter was miraculously released from prison and came to the house of Mary and John Mark, the maid Rhoda recognized Peter at the door and reported to those praying inside the house. In their disbelief they exclaimed, "You are out of your mind!" (Acts 12:15).

In the Scriptures, demon possession was usually considered the reason for mental disorders. Today there still are those who would erroneously suggest that mental health issues are a sign of a supernatural spiritual evil or a sinful nature. I knew a woman who suffered from major depression. She believed that she was beyond salvation because this depression was, in her mind, a sign that she was "full of the devil and dammed to hell." Sadly she was told exactly that by her pastor. Her church attempted to exorcise the demons in her to no avail, plunging her into even more self-destructive depression.

The stigma of evil and shame is perhaps the worst part about a mental health problem. The National Organization on Disability states:

> Since their disabilities [mental illness] are not physically visible, it is hard for others to adjust to unexpected and "different" behaviors. Sadly, most people have limited knowledge about mental illness and may believe some of the myths about it. Some may even fear "catching" mental illness themselves. Because of this they may not know what to do or say, and they turn away in their uncertainty.[3]

Some of the sensational, but very rare occurrences of violence or mass shootings on college campuses and movie theaters add to the fear and stigma associated with mental illness. According to Mental Health Reporting:

Fact 1: The vast majority of people with mental illness are not violent.

Fact 2: The public is misinformed about the link between mental illness and violence.

Fact 3: Inaccurate beliefs about mental illness and violence lead to widespread stigma and discrimination.

Fact 4: The link between mental illness and violence is promoted by the entertainment and news media.[4]

Hospitality

When I served the Deaf congregation in Baltimore, Deaf people with mental health issues were actually told by their therapists to attend church for socialization and community. Blessedly, the church was a supportive place where differences were accommodated and there was acceptance of a wide variety of behaviors.

The good news is there is much that the church can do as it ministers with people who live with mental health issues. Professionals in the field provide medications, psychosocial treatments and therapies, and case management, but the church can bring the all-important personal relationships, spiritual nurture, and support.

One such faith-based program is the MacDonell Children's Services of Houma, Louisiana. United Methodist Women supports this home that provides residential services for boys between the ages of eleven and seventeen with emotional and behavioral disorders. All of the youth have psychiatric diagnoses and a history of abuse. MacDonell strives to provide healing help for mind, body, and spirit.[5]

Helpful Advice

Churches should gear up with facts and understanding about the various issues that mental health challenges present. Here is some helpful advice from the National Organization on Disability:

- Remain non-critical when encountering unusual behavior, giving responses that are supportive of the person.

- Cultivate the ability to listen. Ask the person who in the congregation might be supportive.

- Offer either community or private intercessory prayer.

- Make referrals to professionals, when appropriate.

- Do not deny that the person has serious difficulties that may continue a long time.

- Offer choices of opportunities and tasks in the church appropriate to the person's ability.

- Be sensitive to the fact that physical touch, such as a friendly pat, a hug or squeeze of the hand, affects people differently. Some appreciate the caring, but others find touch threatening.

- Be prepared for anger that has no obvious basis. Try not to take it personally.

- Avoid lecturing, arguments, blame, and acts that increase tension.

- Remember that the person or their family members may be in need but may be reluctant to ask for assistance.[6]

Advocacy

Advocacy can be one of the most important gifts that a faith community can provide. Establishing a support group through the National Alliance on Mental Illness (NAMI) in your church can open the doors to mutual support and outreach for people with mental health issues and their families. Churches can do the time-consuming and all-important work of helping locate housing, employment, and transportation. As government funds continue to be cut, more and more volunteers are needed to help.

Christians also need to take a stand when state and federal dollars for mental health services are on the chopping block. There is power in the pen, telephone, and social media to speak out for people without a voice and to retain these vital services in our government budgets.

Our pastors and church leaders may also be challenged with mental health concerns. We have to be particularly willing to support them in whatever way we can. Rev. Michael W. McKinney, Sr. writes about his experience:

The church leadership, both at the conference and district level, needs to create an environment in which pastors who suffer from mental illness, in any form and level of severity, feel confident that they will get the same support offered for any other illness. My feeling is that the caring and support is presently available, but the affected pastors aren't aware that such care exists. Treating pastors affected by this illness with the respect it deserves will naturally make its way into the congregational level. Eliminating the ugly stigma associated with mental illness requires removing the unfounded fears and anxieties affecting too many people, and replacing those negative feelings with the true love of Jesus Christ.[7]

Embodying the true love of Jesus Christ! That is our goal. That is how we must strive to live as we enter into this multifaceted and very human world of mental health.

Chapter 10
Family Issues and Long-term Support

Family Caregiving

In Henri Nouwen's book *Adam, God's Beloved*, he tells about Adam, a man who had severe physical and cognitive challenges from birth. Nouwen writes, "Adam's parents loved him simply because he was Adam. Yes, they recognized and loved him for himself. Without awareness they also welcomed him as one sent to us by God in utter vulnerability to be an instrument of God's blessing."[1] Adam required constant physical care and vigilance from his family. Unfortunately, he had a particularly bad seizure that landed him in the hospital where a double dose of medication left him with even more debilitating physical problems and he lost much of his ability to get around and direct his own activity.

Nouwen describes the care provided by his family: "Rex [his father] does not say much about the enormous work that caring for . . . Adam required. . . . Lifting, bathing, shaving, feeding, laundry, dressing and undressing, schools and day programs, doctors and specialists—it was a huge task."[2]

Eventually the family had to find a long-term placement for Adam and his brother, who also had a seizure disorder. This was very difficult for these faithful parents, but they knew it would be impossible to care for the young men as they became older.[3]

This tiny window into the life of a family affected by disabilities shows a set of circumstances that hundreds of thousands of families face with their children. Other families include people of all ages who were formerly able-bodied, but have acquired a disability from disease or accident. Many families have loved ones with Alzheimer's disease, which slowly moves the person into a world of degenerative cognitive functioning that is very difficult to navigate. Families living with disabilities are in every congregation, although some may have stopped attending while others do not know that they are welcome.

The Church's Response to Families

Many families with children with disabilities want their children to grow up in a faith community and receive religious education. However, they often report that their needs are not met. I knew a family who regularly brought their daughter, who was deaf, to a United Methodist church; but the church did not provide a sign language interpreter for her. The pastor had this student in his confirmation class for a full year without benefit of any visual communication. This deaf student told me she joined the church to make her parents happy but had no idea what she was promising. The congregation did not understand her situation and, although she was physically present, she was far from the church's ministry.

I also know of many positive examples of churches that provide Sunday school classes that are linguistically and educationally appropriate for children, youth, and adults with disabilities. A growing number of faith communities offer successful classes taught by educators who are familiar with autism and other intellectual and developmental disabilities. Without such programs the parents are relegated to the role of caretaker during worship and Sunday school time, never getting a break for their own spiritual nurture. Instead, they are always playing the roles of advocate, disability educator, and round-the-clock responder. This is an exhausting and often lonely journey. The vast majority of our faith communities are woefully ill-prepared for educational and pastoral responses to people with disabilities or families with long-term care issues. But there are things the church can do.

Providing Support

Spiritual and emotional support is an important aspect of ministry to families. Often the birth of a child with a disability will plunge a family into despair as they ponder the possible reasons this happened and struggle with decisions about care and therapy. My own mother, at the age of eighty-four, still talks about the day she found out I was born blind in one eye. She never received the emotional support or spiritual answers she needed during this time in her life and still harbors a sense of guilt and responsibility. Sadly, at some churches families are actually told that disabilities are linked to parental sin, lack of faith, or divine rejection.[4]

Spiritual needs are varied and many, depending on the situation that presents itself. Families may feel overwhelmed with the multiple demands made on their time and energy. Parents or spouses may feel isolated from relatives and friends who withdraw when a disability becomes a part of the family. Others, however, have worked through their feelings and have a sense of acceptance and well-being. They have reached a place where they can provide support to others on the same journey because of their shared experiences. In each case the church can find ways to understand the needs and provide spiritual, emotional, and physical support.

Support can come in the form of pastoral care, but it should be noted that not every pastor or church volunteer is trained to understand the needs of families with disabilities. Churches need to "take steps to ensure that those who provide counseling in your congregation feel equipped to minister to families with disabilities."[5] Care can come from clergy but also from professionals and lay volunteers who are trained to provide these ministries. **Parish nursing**[6] and **Stephen Ministries**[7] are two available avenues for supplementing the support provided by pastors.

Support groups are a widely used and very effective means of offering encouragement and education. An ecumenical ministry in the Washington, DC area offers a weekly religious education event for children with disabilities, during which the parents meet to exchange ideas and experiences in a formalized support group. Groups like these can invite guest speakers to talk about a particular topic. Some groups are connected to larger national organizations such as the National Alliance on Mental Illness or the Hearing Loss Association of America.

The church can also assist through provision of information. A well-stocked church library of books, magazines, and DVDs can provide up-to-date information and ideas. Resource lists with current websites are also helpful, such as those maintained by the United Methodist Committee on DisAbility Ministries.[8] Internet chats can connect people from all over the world through visual social media such as Skype. Information about state and local programs, educational choices, housing opportunities, transportation programs, long-term care options, employment options, assistive equipment and devices, and any number of self-help tips can be a lifeline for families. Often families find navigating through the government system like "dancing with an elephant."[9]

Congregations can provide parents' nights out and respite care for caregivers, either on their own or as a group of churches. This vitally important time away gives families strength to continue their demanding lives. St. James United Methodist Church in Tampa, Florida, provides this service through a monthly program called "Buddy Break."[10]

Camp Aldersgate in Little Rock, Arkansas, is supported by United Methodist Women. The camp's mission is to be active champions for youth and adults with special needs. They provide respite camps for these youth and adults throughout the year so that family members can get away and have some free time.[11]

"Sanctuary" is a program of the Faith United Methodist Church in Austin, Texas. It is designed to give families caring for family members with Alzheimer's disease an afternoon of free time. The church members provide a program and a meal for twelve to fifteen people each week. Respite, community, and fellowship are all vitally important aspects of this ministry, according to Eleanor Johnson, the director.[12]

Churches can also provide financial assistance for equipment, counseling, camp scholarships, and even home improvements. Sometimes the family needs the services of carpenters and builders who can add ramps to the outside of the home. United Methodist Volunteers in Mission groups across the country have banded together to build wheelchair-accessible ramps for people who otherwise have difficulty leaving their homes. "Ramps of Hope," which operates in the Western Pennsylvania Annual Conference, is such a ministry. They build ramps for families in need of wheelchair accessibility, but the ministry also distributes holiday food baskets to recipients and addresses other unmet needs. Deacon Debbie Hills organized this project that has built ninety-two ramps since April 2010.[13]

Ministry with Siblings

Another important aspect of disability ministry is to give extra attention to children who have a sibling with a disability. Often the able-bodied siblings and their needs take second place to the overwhelming concerns of the child with the disability.

> Brothers and sisters may experience a range of bewildering emotions—struggling to find focused time with their parents, wondering whether they will have to take care of their siblings when they are older, or wanting support, information, and advice from their peers in similar situations.[14]

I participated in a weekend camp experience a number of years ago for families with children with multiple disabilities. The program included a separate group for the typically developing siblings. I learned a great deal from these siblings. Many felt left out and resentful of their siblings who had disabilities. Others were overly responsible, taking a role in the care and protection of their challenged brother or sister at levels of maturity beyond their age. Some expressed the sense that their family was not like other families. They wanted to be accepted by their friends at school but did not know how. It was helpful for them to share their feelings in this group designed for siblings just like them.

United Methodist pastor Rev. Dr. Vicki Gordy-Stith was the able-bodied sister whose brother had an intellectual disability. She reflected on life growing up with Howie: "As a child, I always felt our family was strange. People would stare at us in public and we often didn't do things that 'normal' families did. I never felt like I fit in anywhere. When I looked around, however, I discovered others also existed 'on the margins.' And we could be included together and find great joy as we came to know our own strengths and gifts."[15] Our churches can be places where families can "fit in" and where people on the margins come into the middle as we demonstrate love and acceptance for all.

Support for the Long Haul

One of the most important gifts that churches can give to people with disabilities is friendship for the long haul. When a congregation offers long-term, unconditional friendship to a family struggling with chronic care of a loved one, there is strength and help that is a "balm in Gilead." Too often in our busy world, church members are happy to help for a season but then go on to the next thing and leave the family and the person with the disability alone. People don't mean to be thoughtless, but when visits and phone calls stop there is a sense of isolation and abandonment that hurts beyond words.

John Hunt Kinnaird, a man who had suffered from paralysis as well as some brain injury, described this in a poem:

*Sometimes we make friends and for ten days,
or nine weeks, or longer, we are close
But then it's funny how you forget us
While we remember you.*[16]

In a church that I served there was a husband and wife who felt the long-term supportive friendship of their church community. The husband developed Alzheimer's disease and for twenty years his wife faithfully cared for him at home until the day she could no longer lift him. At that point he was moved to a nursing facility. This family was surrounded by a team of faithful friends from the Lansdowne United Methodist Women who made a pact to call the wife every day. They also came to visit, purchased briefs, gave her time away from her husband, and always remembered birthdays and holidays.

Every church, no matter how large or small, can be in ministry with families who have loved ones with disabilities.

Chapter 11
Veterans with Disabilities

Facts and Figures

According to one source, there are 21.5 million military veterans in the United States. Of that number, 3.5 million veterans have a service-connected disability rating and more than 800,000 have severe disabilities.[1]

War injuries vary with the conflict and the environment, and the type of weapons and armor used determines the kind of injuries that are typically suffered. In our most recent conflicts in Iraq and Afghanistan there has been a widespread use of improvised bombs. According to a May 2012 Associated Press article, body armor that protects soldiers from these bombs allows many to survive injuries that would have been fatal in the past. This article lists other injuries experienced in these recent wars:

- More than 1,600 of [veterans who have sought care] lost a limb, many others lost fingers or toes.

- At least 156 are blind, and thousands of others have impaired vision.

- More than 177,000 have hearing loss, and more than 350,000 report tinnitus—noise or ringing in the ears.

- Thousands are disfigured, as many as 200 of them so badly that they may need face transplants. One-quarter of battlefield injuries requiring evacuation include wounds to the face or jaw, one study found. . . .

Others have invisible wounds. More than 400,000 of these new veterans have been treated by the VA [veteran's administration] for a mental health problem, most commonly, PTSD [post-traumatic stress disorder].

Tens of thousands of veterans suffered traumatic brain injury, or TBI—mostly mild concussions from bomb blasts—and doctors don't know what's in store for them long term.[2]

Contemporary Issues: PTSD, Sexual Trauma, Suicide

For the most part these wounded veterans are young people who were healthy and in the prime of life prior to their war injuries. This is a unique community of people with disabilities with a unique set of needs and family concerns. Many must make a long-term adjustment to a drastically different life than their life prior to deployment and injury. This is a place where the church needs to be involved.

One spouse of a veteran writes:

> When my U.S. Navy SEAL husband returned from Iraq with only a broken leg, I praised God that he was home safe and sound. In the months that followed his homecoming, I sensed that his leg was the least of our concerns. Although he was recovering physically, his soul still walked with a limp. His unseen wounds, caused by war zone experiences, went unmentioned, unnoticed and untreated. Slowly but surely, these invisible injuries infected our marriage, our children and our family life. He was home with us in body but in his spirit a war still raged. From irritability and irrationality to nightmares and emotional paralysis, it became very clear to me that my veteran husband was suffering from posttraumatic stress. For two years my husband denied any need for help and unintentionally led our family into a land of silent suffering."[3]

Our veterans are both male and female. Even though females in the military up until now did not participate in combat, 14.6 percent of active duty forces in the United States military and 13 percent of the veterans of the conflict in Iraq and Afghanistan are women. Common diagnoses are PTSD, depression, and hypertension. At least 20 percent indicate that they have experienced sexual harassment or assault. The Caregivers and Veterans Omnibus Health Services Act of 2010 aims to improve health care of female veterans.[4]

It should be noted that Military Sexual Trauma can be man-to-woman, but also woman-to-man, woman-to-woman, or man-to-man. Military sexual trauma can also lead to PTSD. Every VA facility has a Military Sexual Trauma coordinator who can provide treatment and specialized outpatient mental health services.[5]

Suicide is another tragedy of war that is not only found among active duty soldiers but among veterans as well. An August 2012 *Christian Science Monitor* article recounts the tragic story of a twenty-five-year-old Iraq veteran who unexpectedly shot himself in his own backyard, with his father nearby but unable to react in time. According to this same article, the rate of suicide among veterans from the Iraq and Afghanistan wars is higher than for active duty service members. The Pentagon report released in January 2012 noted that "approximately 950 veterans under VA care attempted suicide each month between October 2008 and December 2010." One source commented that the two things that most suicides have in common are alcohol and a gun.[6]

Church Response

The church has been responding to the huge need that veterans with disabilities have and this need will continue to escalate as the conflict in Afghanistan winds down and more military personnel return home. "The Lazarus Project" is such an effort that is run by the Wesley Foundation of Austin Peay State University, which is not far from the Fort Campbell Army Post. The goal of this project is to "support veterans and their families on campus by providing free counseling, support groups, and other services." Approximately 1,500 students at this university are veterans or family members of service personnel. The project began when many of them sought mental health services at Fort Campbell, only to be told that there were only enough counselors to take care of the active military personnel. Rev. Jodi McCullah from the Wesley Foundation applied for and was awarded a grant from the Tennessee Annual Conference Committee on Mercy and Missions. They use the funds to provide counseling as well as to organize support groups for military spouses and art classes for their children. One veteran reported that the Lazarus Project was responsible for saving his marriage after he was able to get help for panic attacks and other stress-related issues.[7]

Rev. Laura Bender is a United Methodist chaplain in the Navy who also serves as chaplain for the Wounded Warriors Marine unit. This unit carries out all administrative and nonmedical care for injured and ill Marines. Bender emphasizes that "one of the greatest wounds is the soul wound."[8] She recounts a conversation with a veteran who was struggling with the memory of having killed a child while he was serving in the military. Those kinds of memories make persons wonder if they are really welcome at church, and if God still hears their prayers and loves them. "I think addressing soul wounds is one of the major areas that the church needs to figure ways to get at, and certainly it is something that I, as a chaplain, spend a good deal of time working with service members about," says Bender.[9]

Jenny Sullivan is program manager for the Warrior Athlete Reconditioning Program, a Marine Corps program. A United Methodist, she is a veteran herself who was wounded in combat. She says that athletic events for veterans with mobility challenges "give them an opportunity to be competitive, to have people cheering them on, to have something to take their minds off their injuries."[10] She urges the church to work with veterans with disabilities. "They're not gonna grow their limb back and they're not gonna always recover from an injury 100 percent and so they're always gonna need the support. I just don't want people to forget about 'em."[11]

Churches can also be in ministry with families of soldiers who died in battle and lift up the sacrifices of military service personnel during special events in the life of the church. First UMC of Lancaster, Pennsylvania, held a Veteran's Day service during worship. They also collected thank-you notes that were sent to the VA hospital in Lebanon, Pennsylvania, or to local veterans with disabilities. Rev. William Lentz, the pastor of First United Methodist Church, offered prayers for all of the armed service men and women and reminded all to give thanks to them as they "put their lives on the line for an ideal, for a hope or for a vision of the future."[12]

The United Methodist Endorsing Agency of the General Board of Higher Education and Ministry—the agency responsible for chaplaincy—offers suggestions for congregations that can be adapted to meeting the needs of veterans with disabilities and their families:

1. Educate the congregation about typical issues as well as resources available.

2. Keep the service members, injured veterans, and their families in prayer. Keep them on the church mailing list so they feel a part of their church home.

3. Attend or sponsor departure and welcome-home events when feasible.

4. Support family members proactively and follow-through on needs that families share. This may include practical assistance with household and yard tasks that can be overwhelming.

5. Be aware of the emotional toll that separation and injury take, and refer for professional counseling if needed. Utilize resources such as Stephen Ministries and local interfaith groups.

6. Offer support groups for spouses, with child care available during the meetings. Consider offering a Bible study for veterans as an outlet and support group as well as a way to help veterans work through faith issues related to their deployment and experiences.

7. Create a Circle of Care for families and individuals that need extra and consistent support.

8. Stay patient and persistent, realizing that trust takes time to establish.[13]

The human touch, care and concern, resources and accessibility—these are all gifts that the body of Christ can bring to veterans with disabilities as they make adjustment to life after war. In turn, these veterans can bring a depth of life experiences and new ideas to congregations. The United Methodist Church can be proud of the many ways it supports our service members. There are many good resources on the United Methodist Higher Education and Ministry website for churches interested in exploring additional ideas.[14] The ministry possibilities are endless.

Chapter 12
Ordained Ministry

Ordained and Retired the Same Year: Struggles to "Get In"

Rev. David Seymour prepared to serve in The United Methodist Church as a pastor with cerebral palsy (CP). His CP affected his motor skills and physical coordination. As a result he used a wheelchair for mobility. His abilities to think and reason were intact. Seymour felt a call to the ordained ministry as a young person and pursued this calling by going to seminary and following the denomination's protocol for ordination. After graduation he was not offered an appointment in the year that he was to be ordained. The Board of Ordained Ministry agreed to ordain him as an elder on the condition that he agree to retire at the same time. He has never been allowed to serve nor has he received financial support or pension.[1]

Seymour writes: "For over 20 years I have endured the Conference Board of Ordained Ministry's mistreatment of me. I was deeply hurt by the ruling and its aftermath. Today, it still stings."[2]

Ordination in The United Methodist Church

How can such decisions be made in The United Methodist Church? Are there limitations placed on who can serve as pastors? As a denomination we preach inclusiveness, stating, "Inclusiveness means openness, acceptance, and support that enables all persons to participate in the life of the Church, the community, and the world; therefore, inclusiveness denies every semblance of discrimination."[3]

We further state that "in The United Methodist Church inclusiveness means the freedom for the total involvement of all persons who meet the requirements of The United Methodist *Book of Discipline* in the membership and leadership of the Church at any level and in every place. In the spirit of this declaration, United Methodist seminaries will make all efforts to meet Americans with Disabilities (ADA) accessibility standards by the year 2011."[4]

One does not need special physical or sensory abilities in order to carry out the calling of an ordained minister, which include "ordained ministers are called by God to a lifetime of servant leadership in specialized ministries among the people of God. Ordained ministers are called to interpret to the Church the needs, concerns, and hopes of the world and the promise of God for creation."[5]

Thus The United Methodist Church affirms the gifts and graces of all people, no matter their abilities, as participants, lay leaders, and ordained leaders. A disability should not disqualify one for consideration for ordination and any other leadership positions in the church. As long as a person with a disability meets the requirements, she or he should be treated the same as an able-bodied person with regard to appointments and leadership opportunities.[6]

Common Challenges

Seymour's experience is not unique. A conference Board of Ordained Ministry may be reluctant to vote for the ordination of a person with a disability. A local congregation may not want to accept a pastor with a disability because of fear, ignorance, or their unwillingness to make the necessary accommodations for the pastor to be successful. I am familiar with a church that would not accept the appointment of a pastor who used a wheelchair for mobility unless the conference was willing to pay for the accessibility renovations of the parsonage.

Bishops and cabinets may be unable or unwilling to appoint a person with a disability to a church for a variety of reasons. I know of a pastor with a vision challenge who was approved by the Board of Ordained Ministry for ordination but simply did not make it on the appointment list that year. Only when there was an outcry from the seminary and members of the Board of Ordained Ministry was an appointment devised for this pastor as an assistant to a circuit of churches. At times bishops and cabinets recommend that people with disabilities apply for disability benefits and seek an inactive status because there is not an appointment that would work for them given the openings that are available that year. Some pastors with disabilities are asked to accept a less-than-full-time appointment. Finding an appropriate placement can be difficult for a variety of reasons and not necessarily be the result of discrimination. However, we as the church need to strive to provide economic justice for all people and make the additional efforts to lift up the giftedness of pastors with disabilities.

The appointment of a pastor with a disability raises similar issues to those that sometimes arise when cross-cultural appointments are made or a church receives its first female pastor. Human nature is such that people do not always appreciate the gift that diversity brings to the church. Congregations may prefer a pastor from their cultural background whose profile fits their traditional expectations. Disability crosses all cultural and gender lines, making it unique and yet similar in the challenges it presents.

The Need to Prove and Explain Oneself

Rev. Thomas Coughlin was the first Deaf ordained Roman Catholic priest in the United States. He was ordained in 1970 after a long journey of training and preparation. Coughlin explained that during the process he had to face a number of realities that are common to all pastors with disabilities. He said that church officials in authority over the ordination of people with disabilities often have misconceptions about the abilities and qualifications of the candidate. This can lead to fear and sometimes rejection. Very often people with disabilities have to work twice as hard as able-bodied people to accomplish the same tasks. Educational accommodations often take more time, cost more money, and require additional study. Frequently people with disabilities have to "pass" for able-bodied as much as possible to be acceptable to churches and church officials. In Coughlin's case, he had to speak with his voice and lip-read when his preferred language was that of American Sign Language (ASL). Overfunctioning in order to comply with the able-bodied world's expectations is a common experience for pastors with disabilities.[7]

I have noted while working with interns who are deaf that people with disabilities are constantly explaining their disability to new people, church officials included. They are in a position of always teaching the world the basics about their condition as well as their needed accommodations. This can be exhausting.

Rev. Dr. Kirk VanGilder, an elder in the Baltimore-Washington Conference who is Deaf, uses ASL, and identifies with Deaf culture explains: "It's not an active discrimination but a weariness of having to continually explain oneself over and over and answer questions about things others generally don't have to about their cultural identity. You end up spending so much time explaining your identity that you never get to be 'just you.'"[8]

In every situation a new pastor with a disability has to prove herself or himself in order to be accepted. Some people in the church are never won over no matter their exposure or education, as past experience and personal prejudices run deep. Nonetheless, many people with disabilities are serving effectively and bring to ministry unique and powerful gifts that are needed for the body of Christ to be its most vibrant witness to the world. People with disabilities can function just as well as able-bodied people. They can do so by having the necessary accommodations and by partnering with a congregation that appreciates the equal humanity of all people.

Gifts from the Disability Experience

Sometimes pastors with disabilities bring deep reservoirs of insight and strength that only a disability can bring. Rev. Victoria Schlintz, a United Methodist pastor from California who has amyotrophic lateral sclerosis (Lou Gehrig's disease), explains that the disease itself has brought her a number of gifts. She finds she has a broader perspective that is less centered on herself and more in alignment with the divine. Her disability has helped her determine what really matters and how she can best live out her values. She has been forced to contemplate suffering and has realized that God walks alongside her during her trials rather than eliminating the difficulties. As a result, she strongly believes that God's grace is more than sufficient for her and for those whose faith is strengthened through her witness and experiences.[9]

Strategies for the Church Moving Forward

How can the church be a more welcoming recipient of the gifts of pastors with disabilities? There are many ways. Congregations and church members can:

1. Learn as much as possible about people with disabilities, their accommodations and the gifts they bring to a church through training events, studies and **disability awareness** worship services.

2. Find ways to provide physical accommodations as well as spiritual support and to overcome stereotypes and negative attitudes

3. Continue to encourage people with disabilities to consider their calling into the ordained ministry. For instance, young adults with disabilities who are sensing a call can attend the Exploration event held biennially by the United Methodist General Board of Higher Education and Ministry. A wide range of accommodations is always provided.

4. Support the pastor's participation in the United Methodist Association of Ministers with Disabilities and other groups where ideas and mutual support can be shared.

5. Encourage and lift up laypeople with disabilities as leaders, realizing that many lay leaders eventually are called to the ordained ministry.

The church has much to learn from its pastors with disabilities.

Chapter 13
Conclusion and Commencement

There is much more that could be said about disabilities and the church. This book is merely an appetizer, an introduction, and a megaphone shouting loud encouragement for churches and faith communities to engage in ministry with people with disabilities. Other issues that need to be explored are those concerning people with chemical sensitivities, dietary challenges, chronic fatigue syndrome, chronic pain, allergies, and small stature. The world outside the United States in developing countries also includes millions of people who are even more severely marginalized by poverty and lack of access to medical care, meaningful employment, and education. Many people with disabilities around the globe suffer in silence from an even bigger stigma of shame than is experienced here in the United States.

I invite you to get busy in your church and establish a new or invigorated ministry with people with disabilities. Every church can be a place of true accessibility and empowerment.

The Reverend Dr. Eric Pridmore, a United Methodist minister who is blind, tells about his life growing up in a United Methodist church this way:

> Fortunately for me, my family was very involved in a local United Methodist congregation. Outside my own home, the church was one of the only social settings where I felt at home. Virtually, I had no friends in middle school or high school; however, my church youth group, comprised of about ten members, was a place where I found acceptance and inclusion. These youth became my friends at a time when I urgently needed them. I found acceptance and inclusion in a way that I had never before experienced; consequently, the church as a whole became a home for me—a place of safety and peace in the midst of numerous physical, emotional and social struggles. The youth and adults of my congregation were as Christ to me, giving me acceptance, inclusion, peace and hope. The church was a true means of grace for me, helping to save my life at a time of deep despair and loneliness.[1]

Like Pridmore's home church, every congregation has the potential for being a life-giving and empowering haven for people with disabilities. However, people with disabilities are often missing from our churches despite the gospel mandate to "go therefore and make disciples of all nations" (Matthew 28:19). Churches miss out on a marvelous opportunity when they neglect the inclusion of this gifted community. Disability ministry is possible in every church, no matter the size or location. Here are some practical steps to begin the journey.

Practical Steps for the Journey

Begin with prayer. The Book of James reminds us: "The prayer of the righteous is powerful and effective" (5:16b). Gather a group of people for a time of intentional prayer for a potential disability ministry. Prayer unleashes the power of God in this world and accomplishes great things. Sometimes we rush into a program without the prayer foundation and find a lack of focus and resources. Prayer provides the road map for the next steps and the means to accomplish these ministries. A prayerful beginning takes time, but is essential.

Enlarge this prayer group into a committee that includes people who believe that God has called them to serve in this ministry. The committee should also invite the pastor(s). The pastoral leaders must be supportive of this work or it will not be successful. Sadly, through the years I have encountered pastors who either are uncomfortable being with people who have disabilities or object to a request for needed changes in the way worship operates in order to achieve access. I have met more than one pastor who insisted that the sign language interpreter be put in the back of the sanctuary because they thought that the interpreter distracted people from full attention to the sermon.

The committee also should include key leaders of the church who are responsible for programmatic ministries, finances, and building matters. Most importantly, people with disabilities need to be active participants. Most faith communities have at least one person with a disability who could contribute; if not, the committee should seek out someone from the community to participate. There is no integrity in the process otherwise. Family members of persons with disabilities are helpful in communicating the needs of those who provide daily supportive care.

In addition, it is helpful to include members from your congregation or the community such as a teacher in an inclusive education program, a social worker who specializes in disabilities, a rehabilitation therapist, and others from the medical profession. You may want to invite a family or volunteers from a church that has a successful disability ministry.

The committee should begin with an accessibility audit of the church. There are a many audits available. The United Methodist Committee on DisAbility Ministries' website provides a number of options.[2] The audit could take several weeks to complete but this time should be used to carefully analyze every aspect of the physical and attitudinal accessibility of the church.

Audit committees are often surprised at the little things preventing access that can be changed quickly and inexpensively. The direction that a door swings, the location of the toilet paper, or the placement of an additional handrail can make a huge difference. After a thorough accessibility audit, committee members are often confronted with a staggering number of previously overlooked challenges that will take a good deal of effort and money to change. Some of these barriers include high-pile carpet, which challenges safe mobility, a raised chancel with no wheelchair access so that only able-bodied people can lead in worship, poor lighting caused by many ornate stained-glass windows that prevent access for people with low vision, and an old public address system that does not allow for assistive listening devices. All of the findings should be recorded and shared with the committee and church members for their feedback.

Once the review is completed, the committee should prayerfully determine next steps. The ministry needs to be primarily people-based and not building-renovation driven. I remember teaching a workshop some years ago at a large metropolitan church and asking, "Who do you already have in your church with a disability who could be better served?" They replied, "We don't have anyone with disabilities attending our church." Then one person sheepishly spoke up: "Well, we do have Rick" (not his real name). I inquired further and found that Rick was a teenager with developmental disabilities and a hearing loss who had been attending church with his grandmother for worship every Sunday for more than ten years. There was nothing provided for him in the way of ministry or inclusion. He had been right under their noses but he had been invisible. The church agreed to start with Rick and they developed a successful Sunday school class for people with intellectual disabilities.

At the same time the church should begin a systematic plan for making the building as physically accessible as possible. People have often told me they don't need to go to the expense of building a ramp because no one uses a wheelchair at their church. People who use wheelchairs for mobility will not come unless there is a ramp and at any time any one of the able-bodied people of the church could find herself or himself in need of a ramp.

I know of a church that decided to build a ramp for a child with a mobility challenge. The project was fought by the board of trustees and the finance committee because the attendance of this child was sporadic at best. The ramp was built nonetheless, and within a year the head trustee who had strongly objected had a stroke and needed to use a wheelchair. He became the person who used the ramp the most and he experienced a change of heart about the issue of accessibility as a general practice.

The disability committee should begin early on with awareness efforts. Provide an on-going stream of information to the church members about the issues around disability ministry and the progress of the committee work. Some suggestions include a sermon series about disabilities, newsletter and bulletin articles, a Disability Awareness Sunday, a disability workshop, a guest preacher who has a disability, or a Bible study devoted to difficult passages that deal with disabilities. The church website should be made accessible for persons with low vision who use a screen reader, and include information on the location of accessible parking and entrances as well as accommodations provided. In addition, put concrete plans in place to provide the kinds of access that the audit calls for. It is impossible to do everything at one time, but a committee that meets regularly and faithfully can, with help of a good checklist, accomplish much.

Once you have programs and access in place, begin to reach out into the community as the Spirit guides you. No matter what direction this committee decides to go, the ultimate goal should always be empowerment. People with disabilities should be intentionally included in all aspects of the church's leadership and decision making. They should be participants in the worship and ministry activities and not just spectators. Paternalistic oppression is at work when people with disabilities are "taken care of" and given a "special' seat in the sanctuary but nothing more. Accomplishing **full participation** includes leadership and socialization and takes additional steps of awareness-building and barrier removal.

A final word: a church with a flourishing ministry with people with disabilities will spend a good bit of money on accessibility and programs to be truly successful. Financial realities should not be allowed to dictate the ministry. With a prayer-covered solid plan as a foundation, the money will come. Money follows ministry. As the congregation begins to experience the benefits and the joy of including everyone in the life of the church, hearts and pocketbooks will open.

Deaconess Charmaine Cothran is the director of "African Americans Living with Multiple Sclerosis" in Chicago, Illinois. She has multiple sclerosis (MS) herself, and others living with the disease find that her personal journey with MS is a double blessing as she walks the walk with them. Cothran's program includes monthly meetings that feature opportunities for socialization, resource sharing, and friendship. In addition she provides spiritual support and encouragement for family members who care for their loved ones. She helps educate the church and the world about the challenges and the hope for people with

MS, and she engages the church to partner in this ministry with her. The goal of Cothran's program is to help people with MS realize that they can move forward and live life to the fullest. Their motto is "We're doing the best we can, while we can, for as long as we can."[3]

This is what it means to have a ministry of awareness, accessibility, and advocacy. The ministries of United Methodist Women and The United Methodist Church are bringing the love and hope of Christ to many. You will be blessed as you open the door of your congregation to people with disabilities.

Endnotes

About the Cover

1. Graphic Artists Guild, "Downloadable Disability Access Symbols," accessed October 2, 2013, https://www.graphicartistsguild.org/tools_resources/downloadable-disability-access-symbols.
2. Oregon State University, "Web Accessibility," accessed October 2, 2013, http://oregonstate.edu/accessibility/web.
3. Clipartlogo.com, "Guide dog clip art," accessed October 4, 2013, http://www.clipartlogo.com/image/guidedog-clip-art_393970.html.
4. FOH Online, "Sound Sanctuary: Can You Hear Me?" September 2013, https://www.graphicartistsguild.org/tools_resources/downloadable-disability-access-symbols.
5. The Queen's Theatre, "Access Logos," accessed October 2, 2013, http://www.queens-theatre.co.uk/legacy/access/logos.htm.
6. iStock, "Accessibility Icons," accessed October 2, 2013, http://www.istockphoto.com/stock-illustration-14871604-accessibility-icons-white-series.php.
7. Sara Hendren and Brian Glenney, "The Accessible Icon Project," accessed October 2, 2013, http://www.accessibleicon.org.

Introduction

1. Peggy A. Johnson, "Be Thou My Vision," in *Speaking Out: Gifts of Ministering Undeterred by Disabilities,* Robert L. Walker, ed. (Charleston: CreateSpace, Inc., 2012), 43-44.
2. Ibid., 44.
3. Ibid., 44-45.
4. Ibid., 47.

Chapter 1: Awareness

1. Mitchell M. Galloway, "Walking by Faith," in *Speaking Out: Gifts of Ministering Undeterred by Disabilities,* Robert L. Walker, ed. (Charleston: CreateSpace, Inc., 2012), 104.
2. Ibid., 107.
3. Disability Funders Network, "Disability Stats and Facts," 2012, http://www.disabilityfunders.org/disability-stats-and-facts.
4. World Health Organization, *World Report on Disability* (Geneva, Switzerland: WHO Press, 2011), 3. http://whqlibdoc.who.int/publications/2011/9789240685215_eng.pdf.
5. Ibid., 29.
6. Disabled World, "ADA 20th Anniversary US Disability Facts and Statistics," July 19, 2010, http://www.disabled-world.com/disability/statistics/ada-anniversary.php.
7. *World Report on Disability,* 3.
8. "The Social Community: Rights of Persons with Disabilities," *The Book of Discipline of the United Methodist Church, 2012* (Nashville: The United Methodist Publishing House, 2012), ¶162.I.
9. Kessler Foundation/NOD, "The ADA, 20 Years Later," July 2010, http://www.2010disabilitysurveys.org/pdfs/surveyresults.pdf, 128-130.
10. Evelyn McDonald, "What? And She's Disabled, Too?" in *Speaking Out: Gifts of Ministering Undeterred by Disabilities,* 112-113.
11. "Accessibility Audits," United Methodist Committee on DisAbility Ministries, last updated June, 2013, http://www.umdisabilityministries.org/2410.html.

Chapter 2: The Bible and Disabilities

1. Amos Yong, *The Bible, Disability and the Church: A New Vision of the People of God* (Grand Rapids: William B. Eerdmans Publishing, 2011), 57.
2. Ibid., 57.
3. *New York Annual Conference Journal* (1997), 8-19.
4. Peggy A. Johnson, "Be Thou My Vision," in *Speaking Out: Gifts of Ministering Undeterred by*

Disabilities, Robert L. Walker ed. (Charleston: CreateSpace, Inc., 2012), 47.

5   Joni Eareckson, *Joni, The Unforgettable Story of a Young Woman's Struggle Against Quadriplegia and Depression* (Grand Rapids: Zondervan Publishing House, 1976), 68-69.

6   Melissa Lauber, "Overview: Conference Adopts Bold 2020 Vision" *UM Connection – Baltimore Washington Conference,* 23, No. 6, (2012), 12.

7   Rev. Len Calhoun, interview by author, 11/26/12.

8   Donna Baker, Congo Partnership "Cataract Surgical Team." http://www.pen-del.org/pages/detail/642.

9   Catholic Communications, Sydney Archdiocese "World's Only Deaf-Blind Priest Inspires Sydneysiders," 8/1/12, http://www.sydneycatholic.org/news/latest_news/2012/201281_616shtml.

10 Jonathan Campbell, "A Journey to Wholeness," in *Speaking Out: Gifts of Ministering Undeterred by Disabilities,* 185.

11 Beth Hopkins, "Why I Don't Need Your Faith-Healing," 9/4/12, http://www.huffingtonpost.com/beth-hopkins/i-dont-need-your-faith-healing_b_1844656.html.

12 Jennie Weiss Block, *Copious Hosting: A Theology of Access for People with Disabilities* (New York: Continuum, 2002), 153-154.

13 Gustavo Gutiérrez, *Theology of Liberation.* 15th anniversary edition (New York: Orbis, 1988), xiii.

14 Kyle Aiken Forder, interview by author, 8/21/12.

15 ADA Publications, "Americans with Disabilities Act of 1990, As Amended," updated 3/25/09, http://www.ada.gov/pubs/ada.htm.

16 Ann Rose Davie and Ginny Thornburgh, *That All May Worship: An Interfaith Welcome to People with Disabilities,* Ginny Thornburgh, ed., 6th printing (Washington, DC: National Organization on Disability, 2000), 50.

17 Deborah Beth Creamer, *Disability and Christian Theology: Embodied Limits and Constructive Possibilities* (New York: Oxford University Press, 2009), 76.

18 Scott Vickery, interview by author, 2/15/13.

Chapter 3: Labels and Etiquette

1   *Merriam-Webster's Collegiate Dictionary, Eleventh Edition* (Springfield, MA: Merriam-Webster, 2004), 3.

2   Ron Amundson, "About the Meaning of "Handicap," updated 2006, http://www.uhh.hawaii.edu/~ronald/HandicapDefinition.htm.

3   Texas Council for Developmental Disabilities, "People First Language," December 2011, http://tcdd.texas.gov/resources/people-first-language.

4   Candice M. Tate and Scott Adams, "Appendix B: Cultural Definitions of Deafness. "Information Gaps on the Deaf and Hard of Hearing Population: A Background Paper," May 2006, 30-31, www.wiche.edu/info/publications/InformationGapsResearchPaper.pdf.

5   Words by Maltbie D. Babcock, *The United Methodist Hymnal* (Nashville: The United Methodist Publishing House, 1989), 144.

6   Ibid., 57.

7   Angela Orlando, "Poster Child," http://dotbug3.blogspot.com/2012/05/poster-child.html. Used by permission.

8   Irene M. Ward and Associates, *The Ten Commandments of Communicating with People with Disabilities DVD* (New York: Program Development Associates, 2007) www.disabilitytraining.com.

9   Charlotte Shepard, Wineva Hankamer, and Devorah Greenstein, "Communication and Etiquette with Persons with Disabilities," United Methodist Committee on DisAbility Ministries, April 2009, http://www.umdisabilityministries.org/download/10_etiquette.pdf.

Chapter 4: Deaf Culture

1. National Association of the Deaf, "Public Accommodations," retrieved 07/21/13, http://www.nad.org/issues/civil-rights/ada/public-accommodations.
2. Hannah Lewis, *Deaf Liberation Theology* (Burlington: Ashgate Publishing Co., 2007), 31.
3. Candice M. Tate and Scott Adams, "Appendix B: Cultural Definitions of Deafness. "Information Gaps on the Deaf and Hard of Hearing Population: A Background Paper," May 2006, 30, www.wiche.edu/info/publications/InformationGapsResearchPaper.pdf.
4. Tom Hudspeth, interview with author, 7/12/12.
5. "Public Accommodations."
6. Glenn Collins, "The Family; Children of Deaf Share their Lives." The New York Times: December 15, 1986. www.wiche.edu/info/publications/InformationGapsResearchPaper.pdf.
7. Elke Sharma, "Mission of Deaf Hands and Hearts," *The United Methodist Women News* 4, No. 1, 5.

Chapter 5: Hard of Hearing and Late-Deafened

1. Nancy Kingsley, interview with author, 12/1/12.
2. Hearing Loss Association of America, "Living with Hearing Loss," 2013, http://www.hearingloss.org/content/living-hearing-loss.
3. Neil Bauman, "Speechreading (Lip-Reading)" Center for Hearing Loss Help, http://www.hearinglosshelp.com/articles/speechreading.htm.
4. Ann Rose Davie and Ginny Thornburgh, *That All May Worship: An Interfaith Welcome to People with Disabilities,* Ginny Thornburgh, ed., 6th printing (Washington DC: National Organization on Disability, 2000), 25.
5. National Institute on Deafness and Other Communication Disorders, "Quick Statistics," 6/16/10, http://www.nidcd.nih.gov/health/statistics/Pages/quick.aspx.
6. William Barclay, *Prayers for Help and Healing* (HarperSanFrancisco, 1968), 57. Reprinted by permission of HarperCollins Publishers Ltd. © 1968, William Barclay.
7. "Quick Statistics."
8. United Methodist Communications, "2010 State of the Church: Congregational Life Survey" http://www.umc.org/site/c.lwL4KnN1LtH/b.6072841/k.7ACF/2010_State_of_the_Church_Congregational_Life_Survey.htm#.Uev0tY2TiO0.
9. Nancy Jill Hale, "The Healing of Acceptance," in *Speaking Out: Gifts of Ministering Undeterred by Disabilities,* Robert L. Walker, ed. (Charleston: CreateSpace, Inc. 2012), 95.
10. "Living with Hearing Loss."
11. Thomas H. Hudspeth, "God Doesn't Call Half of You . . . God Calls ALL of You," in *Speaking Out: Gifts of Ministering Undeterred by Disabilities,* 135.

Chapter 6: Vision Loss

1. American Foundation for the Blind, "Facts and Figures on Adults with Vision Loss, updated January 2013, http://www.afb.org/section.aspx?SectionID=15&TopicID=413&DocumentID=4900.
2. American Foundation for the Blind, "Children and Youth with Vision Loss, updated January 2013, http://www.afb.org/section.aspx?SectionID=15&TopicID=411&DocumentID=4896.
3. Valentin Haüy Association, "Blindness and Visual Impairment: The Statistics," updated 7/18/13, http://www.avh.asso.fr/rubrics/association/statistics.php?langue=eng.
4. World Health Organization, "Visual impairment and blindness," June 2012, http://www.who.int/mediacentre/factsheets/fs282/en/.

5 Charlie Web, "Eye Conditions and Disorders," 2005, http://www.99main.com/~charlief/vi/disorders.html.

6 Ann Rose Davie and Ginny Thornburgh, *That All May Worship: An Interfaith Welcome to People with Disabilities,* Ginny Thornburgh, ed., 6th Printing (Washington DC: National Organization on Disability, 2000), 23-24.

7 Guide Dogs of America, "Meeting a Blind Person or Guide Dog Team," accessed 7/21/13, http://www.guidedogsofamerica.org/1/links-resources/access-etiquette/.

8 Natasha Rashwan, interview with author, 11/23/12.

Chapter 7: Mobility Challenges

1 H. Stephen Kaye, Taewoon Kang, and Mitchell P. LaPlante, "Wheelchair Use in the United States," Disability Statistics Center, Institute for Health and Aging, School of Nursing, University of California, May 2002, http://dsc.ucsf.edu/publication.php.

2 Ann Rose Davie and Ginny Thornburgh, *That All May Worship: An Interfaith Welcome to People with Disabilities,* Ginny Thornburgh, ed., 6th printing (Washington, DC: National Organization on Disability, 2000), 20.

3 BraunAbility, "Disability in America Infographic," updated 06/14/13, http://www.disabled-world.com/disability/statistics/american-disability.php.

4 *That All May Worship,* 21.

5 "Church Accepts Accessibility Audit 'Next Steps' Challenge," *The Voice of the United Methodist Disability Connection,* 2, no. 1 (2012), http://archive.constantcontact.com/fs017/1104745249463/archive/1109131898727.html.

6 *That All May Worship,* 22.

7 Ibid.

8 "Churches Strive for Intentional Hospitality," *The Voice of the United Methodist Disability Connection,* 2, no. 6, (2012), http://archive.constantcontact.com/fs017/1104745249463/archive/1110958172417.html.

9 "Planning and Financial Requirements for Local Church Buildings," *The Book of Discipline of the United Methodist Church, 2012* (Nashville: The United Methodist Publishing House, 2012), ¶2544.

Chapter 8: Cognitive/Intellectual/Developmental Disabilities

1 Matthew 5:3-11.

2 L'Arche, "Charter of the Communities of L'Arche, retrieved 07/21/13, http://www.larche.org/charter-of-the-communities-of-l-arche.en-gb.43.3.content.htm.

3 Henri J. M. Nouwen, *Adam: God's Beloved* (New York: Orbis Books, 2000), 27-28.

4 Disabled World, "Cognitive Disabilities," updated 5/31/13, http://www.disabled-world.com/disability/types/cognitive/.

5 American Association on Intellectual and Developmental Disabilities, "Frequently Asked Questions on Intellectual Disability," 2013, http://aaidd.org/intellectual-disability/definition/faqs-on-intellectual-disability#.UemMco2TiO0.

6 Ibid.

7 Eric W. Carter, *Including People with Disabilities in Faith Communities: A Guide for Service Providers, Families, & Congregations* (Baltimore: Paul H. Brookes Publishing Co., 2007), 119.

8 Ibid., 120-137.

9 Cunningham Children's Home, "United Methodist Women," http://www.cunningham-home.org/umw.htm.

10 Cathy Capo Stone, "Rosa Valdez Early Childhood Learning Center," *United Methodist Women News,* 4, no. 2, (2011), 7, http://new

.gbgm-umc.org/umw/news/articles/item/index.cfm?id=600.

11 *Including People with Disabilities in Faith Communities,* 123-124.

12 Joy Thornburg Melton, "Basic Procedures for Safely Operating Ministries with Older Adults," in *Safe Sanctuaries: The Church Responds to Abuse, Neglect, and Exploitation of Older Adults* (Nashville: Discipleship Resources, 2012), 59-71.

13 Ibid.

14 "u/ability Offers Range of Spiritual Supports and Programs, *The Voice of the United Methodist Disability Connection,* 2, no. 7, (2012), http://archive.constantcontact.com/fs110/1104745249463/archive/1111581677293.html.

15 Jan Snider, "Church Christmas Play Stars Developmentally Disabled Adults," United Methodist News Service, 12/21/04, http://archives.umc.org/interior.asp?ptid=2&mid=6361.

Chapter 9: Mental Health

1 "What Is Mental Illness?" National Alliance on Mental Illness, http://www.nami.org/Template.cfm?Section=By_Illness.

2 "Mental Illness: Facts and Numbers," National Alliance on Mental Illness, http://www.nami.org/factsheets/mentalillness_factsheet.pdf.

3 Ann Rose Davie and Ginny Thornburgh, *That All May Worship: An Interfaith Welcome to People with Disabilities,* Ginny Thornburgh, ed., 6th printing (Washington DC: National Organization on Disability, 2000), 27.

4 Mental Health Reporting, "Facts About Mental Illness and Violence," University of Washington, School of Social Work, http://depts.washington.edu/mhreport/facts_violence.php.

5 MacDonell's Children's Home, "Services," 2101, http://www.macdonellchildren.org.

6 *That All May Worship,* 28.

7 Michael McKinney, "Dancing with Shadows: Serving God in the Dim Light of Mental Illness," in *Speaking Out: Gifts of Ministering Undeterred by Disabilities,* Robert L. Walker, ed. (Charleston: CreateSpace Inc. 2012), 126.

Chapter 10: Family Issues and Long-term Support

1 Henri J. M. Nouwen, *Adam: God's Beloved* (New York: Orbis Books, 2000), 31.

2 Ibid., 27.

3 Ibid.

4 Eric W. Carter, *Including People With Disabilities in Faith Communities: A Guide for Service Providers, Families, & Congregations (*Baltimore: Paul H. Brookes Publishing Co., 2007), 12.

5 Ibid., 145.

6 General Board of Global Ministries, "About Parish/Faith Community Nursing," http://www.gbgm-umc.org/parishnursing/aboutparishnursing.html. Another place to get United Methodist information is http://gbophb.org/cfh/umchmn.asp and for ecumenical information go to http://www.parishnurses.org/.

7 Stephen Ministries, "What Is Stephen Ministry?" 2013, http://www.stephenministries.org/stephenministry/default.cfm/917.

8 United Methodist Committee on DisAbility Ministries, "Learn More: Links to Resources, Organizations, and Technology," accessed 07/21/13, http://www.umdisabilityministries.org/3000.html.

9 Stewart D. Govig, *Strong at the Broken Places: Persons with Disabilities and the Church* (Louisville: John Knox Press, 1989), 64.

10 John Michael De Marco, "Ministry Helps Children with Special Needs, Their Families Feel at Home," *E-review: Florida United Methodist News Service,* 02/08/07, http://www.flumc.info

/cgi-script/csArticles/articles/000032/003208.htm.

11 Camp Aldersgate, "Weekend Camps," 2009, http://www.campaldersgate.net/index.php?option=com_content&view=article&id=16&Itemid=18.

12 Eleanor Johnson, interview with author, 11/25/12.

13 "Ramp Building Ministries," *The Voice of the United Methodist Disability Connection,* 1, no. 5 (2011), http://archive.constantcontact.com/fs017/1104745249463/archive/1106909966699.html. (The number of ramps completed was reported in a telephone conversation with Debbie Hill, July 2013.)

14 *Including People with Disabilities in Faith Communities*, 143-144.

15 Vicki Gordy-Stith, interview with author, 9/20/12.

16 From "Box 257," a poem by John Hunt Kinnaird, in Gene Newman and Joni Eareckson Tada, *All God's Children: Ministry with Disabled Persons* (Grand Rapids: Zondervan Publishing House, 1993), 22.

Chapter 11: Veterans with Disabilities

1 Infoplease, "American Veterans by the Numbers," updated 2012, http://www.infoplease.com/spot/veteranscensus1.html.

2 Marilyn Marchione, "US Faces Surge of New Vets Seeking Disability," 05/28/13, http://www.csmonitor.com/USA/Latest-News-Wires/2012/0528/US-faces-surge-of-new-vets-seeking-disability.

3 Chris Adsit, Rahnella Adsit, Marshéle Carter Waddell, *When War Comes Home: Christ-Centered Healing for Wives of Combat Veterans* (Newport News: Military Ministry Press, 2008), 7.

4 Lily Roberts "We Still Aren't Meeting the Needs of Female Veterans." Next New Deal: The Blog of the Roosevelt Institute, 03/29/12, http://www.nextnewdeal.net/we-still-aren%E2%80%99t-meeting-needs-female-veterans.

5 United States Department of Veterans Affairs, "Military Sexual Trauma," updated 08/05/13, http://www.womenshealth.va.gov/WOMENSHEALTH/trauma.asp.

6 Anna Multrine, "Suicide 'Epidemic' in Army: July Was Worst Month, Pentagon Says," *Christian Science Monitor,* 08/17/12, http://www.csmonitor.com/USA/Military/2012/0817/suicide-epidemic-in-Army-July-was-worst-month-Pentagon-says.

7 Vicki Brown, "Lazarus Project Aims to Help Military Families on Campus," General Board of Higher Education and Ministry, 08/19/10, http://www.gbhem.org/article/lazarus-project-aims-help-military-families-campus#.UdnbKvmTiO0.

8 Kathy L. Gilbert, "Sports Help Warriors on Path to Healing," United Methodist News Service, 01/08/13, http://www.umc.org/site/apps/nlnet/content3.aspx?c=lwL4KnN1LtH&b=5259669&ct=12713193

9 Ibid.

10 Ibid.

11 Ibid.

12 Kathy L. Gilbert, "Church Honors Veterans' Stories of Valor" United Methodist News Service, 11/28/12, http://www.umc.org/site/apps/nlnet/content3.aspx?c=lwL4KnN1LtH&b=5259669&ct=12509571&notoc=1.

13 Bruce Fenner, Tom Carter, Robert Phillips, and Stephen Wall-Smith, Dick Millspaugh, "Congregational Care for Deployed Service members and Their Families," General Board of Higher Education and Ministry, http://www.gbhem.org/article/congregational-care

-deployed-service-members-and-their-families#.UdneYvmTiO0.

14 Laura Bender, "Supporting Military Members & Their Families: A Directory of Organizations and Online Resources," United Methodist Endorsing Agency of the General Board of Higher Education and Ministry, http://www.gbhem.org/sites/default/files/article-attachments/CHAP_SupportingMilFamilies.pdf.

Chapter 12: Ordained Ministry

1 David T. Seymour, "Life with Physical Disabilities, the Christian Life, and the Ordained Ministry," in *Speaking Out: Gifts of Ministering Undeterred by Disabilities,* Robert L. Walker, ed. (Charleston: CreateSpace, Inc., 2012), 224-226.
2 Ibid., 226.
3 "Called to Inclusiveness," *The Book of Discipline of the United Methodist Church, 2012* (Nashville: The United Methodist Publishing House, 2012), ¶140.
4 Ibid.
5 Ibid., "Servant Leadership: Ordained Ministry," ¶139.
6 Ibid., "Qualifications for Election to Provisional Membership," ¶324.8.
7 Sign Enhancers, "Deaf Culture Autobiography Featuring Rev. Thomas Coughlin" (tape), 1989.
8 Kirk A. VanGilder, interview with author, 10/29/12.
9 Victoria Schlintz, "Thorns and More than Sufficient Grace" in *Speaking Out: Gifts of Ministering Undeterred by Disabilities,* 83-87.

Chapter 13: Conclusion and Commencement

1 J. Eric Pridmore, "Seeing the Light: My Journey with Disability" in *Speaking Out: Gifts of Ministering Undeterred by Disabilities,* Robert L. Walker, ed. (Charleston: CreateSpace, Inc., 2012), 161.
2 United Methodist Committee on DisAbility Ministries, "Accessibility Audits," updated June, 2013, http://www.umdisabilityministries.org/2410.html.
3 Charmaine Cothran, interview with author, 02/19/13.

Bibliography

Admundson, Ron. "About the Meaning of 'Handicap." Updated 2006. http://www.uhh.hawaii.edu/~ronald/HandicapDefinition.htm.

Adsit, Chris, Rahnella Adsit, and Marshéle Carter Waddell. *When War Comes Home: Christ-Centered Healing for Wives of Combat Veterans.* Newport News: Military Ministry Press, 2008.

Alexander, Neil, ed. *The Book of Discipline of the United Methodist Church, 2012.* Nashville: The United Methodist Publishing House, 2012.

American Association on Intellectual and Developmental Disabilities. "Frequently Asked Questions on Intellectual Disability." 2013. http://aaidd.org/intellectual-disability/definition/faqs-on-intellectual-disability#.UemMco2TiO0.

American Foundation for the Blind. "Children and Youth with Vision Loss." Updated January 2013. http://www.afb.org/section.aspx?SectionID=15&TopicID=411&DocumentID=4896.

American Foundation for the Blind. "Facts and Figures on Adults with Vision Loss." Updated January 2013. http://www.afb.org/section.aspx?SectionID=15&TopicID=413&DocumentID=4900.

ADA Publications. "Americans with Disabilities Act of 1990, as amended." Updated 3/25/09. http://www.ada.gov/pubs/ada.htm.

Avalos, Hector, Sarah J. Melcher, and Jeremy Schipper, eds., *This Abled Body: Rethinking Disabilities in Biblical Studies.* Atlanta: Society of Biblical Literature, 2007.

Baker, Donna, "Congo Partnership - Cataract Surgical Team." http://www.pen-del.org/pages/detail/642.

Bauman, Neil. "Speechreading (Lip-reading)." Center for Hearing Loss Help. http://www.hearinglosshelp.com/articles/speechreading.htm.

Bender, Laura. "Supporting Military Members & Their Families: A Directory of Organizations and Online Resources." The United Methodist Endorsing Agency of the General Board of Higher Education and Ministry. http://www.gbhem.org/sites/default/files/article-attachments/CHAP_SupportingMilFamilies.pdf.

Block, Jennie Weiss. *Copious Hosting: A Theology of Access for People with Disabilities.* New York: Continuum, 2002.

BraunAbility. "Disability in America Infographic." Updated 06/14/13. http://www.disabled-world.com/disability/statistics/american-disability.php.

Brown, Vicki. "Lazarus Project Aims to Help Military Families on Campus," General Board of Higher Education and Ministry, August 19, 2010. http://www.gbhem.org/article/lazarus-project-aims-help-military-families-campus#.UdnbKvmTiO0.

Campbell, Jonathan. "A Journey to Wholeness." In *Speaking Out: Gifts of Ministering Undeterred by Disabilities.* Robert L. Walker, ed. Charleston: CreateSpace, Inc., 2012; 177-185.

Carter, Eric W. *Including People with Disabilities in Faith Communities: A Guide for Service Providers, Families, & Congregations.* Baltimore: Paul H. Brookes Publishing Co., 2007.

Catholic Communications, Sydney Archdiocese. "World's Only Deaf-Blind Priest Inspires Sydneysiders." August 1, 2012. http://www.sydneycatholic.org/news/latest_news/2012/201281_616.shtml.

"Church Accepts Accessibility Audit 'Next Steps' Challenge." *The Voice of the United Methodist Disability Connection*, 2, no. 1, 2012. http://archive.constantcontact.com/fs017/1104745249463/archive/1109131898727.html.

"Churches Strive for Intentional Hospitality." *The Voice of the United Methodist Disability Connection*, 2, no. 6, 2012. http://archive.constantcontact.com/fs017/1104745249463/archive/1110958172417.html.

Collins, Glenn. "The Family; Children of Deaf Share their Lives." *The New York Times*, December 15, 1986. www.wiche.edu/info/publications/InformationGapsResearchPaper.pdf.

Creamer, Deborah Beth. *Disability and Christian Theology: Embodied Limits and Constructive Possibilities*. New York: Oxford University Press, 2009.

Davie, Ann Rose and Ginny Thornburgh, *That All May Worship: An Interfaith Welcome to People with Disabilities*, Ginny Thornburgh, ed. 6th printing. Washington, DC: National Organization on Disability, 2000.

Davis, Lennard J., ed. *The Disability Studies Reader*. Third edition. New York: Routledge, 2010.

De Marco, John Michael. "Ministry Helps Children with Special Needs, Their Families Feel at Home." *E-review: Florida United Methodist News Service*, February 8. 2007. http://www.flumc.info/cgi-script/csArticles/articles/000032/003208.htm.

Disabled World, "ADA 20th Anniversary US Disability Facts and Statistics," July 19, 2010. http://www.disabled-world.com/disability/statistics/ada-anniversary.php.

Disabled World. "Cognitive Disabilities." Updated 5/31/13. http://www.disabled-world.com/disability/types/cognitive/.

Disability Funders Network. "Disability Stats and Facts." 2012. http://www.disabilityfunders.org/disability-stats-and-facts.

Division of Christian Education of the National Council of the Churches of Christ in the United States of America. *Holy Bible: New Revised Standard Version*. New York: Oxford University Press Inc., 1989.

Eareckson, Joni. *Joni: The Unforgettable Story of a Young Woman's Struggle Against Quadriplegia and Depression*. Grand Rapids: Zondervan Publishing House, 1976.

Eiesland, Nancy L. *The Disabled God: Toward a Liberatory Theology of Disability*. Nashville: Abingdon Press, 1994.

Eiesland, Nancy L. and Don E. Saliers, eds. *Human Disability and the Service of God: Reassessing Religious Practice*. Nashville: Abingdon Press, 1998.

Fenner, Bruce, Tom Carter, Robert Phillips, Stephen Wall-Smith. "Congregational Care for Deployed Service Members and their Families," General Board of Higher Education and Ministry. http://www.gbhem.org/article/congregational-care-deployed-service-members-and-their-families#.UdneYvmTiO0.

Galloway, Mitchell M. "Walking by Faith." In *Speaking Out: Gifts of Ministering Undeterred by Disabilities*. Robert L. Walker, ed. Charleston: Create Space, Inc., 2012; 103-109.

General Board of Global Ministries, "About Parish/Faith Community Nursing." http://www.gbgm-umc.org/parishnursing/aboutparishnursing.html.

Gilbert, Kathy L. "Church Honors Veterans' Stories of Valor." United Methodist News Service. November 28, 2012. http://www.umc.org/site/apps/nlnet/content3.aspx?c=lwL4KnN1LtH&b=5259669&ct=12509571&notoc=1.

Gilbert, Kathy L. "Sports Help Warriors on Path to Healing." United Methodist News Service. January 8, 2013. http://www.umc.org/site/apps/nlnet/content3.aspx?c=lwL4KnN1LtH&b=5259669&ct=12713193.

Govig, Stewart D. *Strong at the Broken Places: Persons with Disabilities and the Church*. Louisville: John Knox Press, 1989.

Gutiérrez, Gustavo. *Theology of Liberation*. 15th Anniversary Edition. New York: Orbis, 1988.

Hale, Nancy Jill. "The Healing of Acceptance." In *Speaking Out: Gifts of Ministering Undeterred by Disabilities*. Robert L. Walker, ed. Charleston: CreateSpace, Inc., 2012; 95-102..

Hearing Loss Association of America. "Living with Hearing Loss." 2013.

http://www.hearingloss.org/content/living-hearing-loss.

Hopkins, Beth. "Why I Don't Need Your Faith-Healing." *Huffington Post*, September 4, 2012. http://www.huffingtonpost.com/beth-hopkins/i-don't-need-your-faith-healing_b_1844656.html

Hudspeth, Thomas H. "God Doesn't Call Half of You . . . God Calls ALL of You." In *Speaking Out: Gifts of Ministering Undeterred by Disabilities*. Robert L. Walker, ed. Charleston: CreateSpace, Inc., 2012; 135-142.

Infoplease. "American Veterans by the Numbers." Updated 2012. http://www.infoplease.com/spot/veteranscensus1.html.

Johnson, Diane Winters. *The View from Under the Pew*. Nashville: Abingdon Press, 2008.

Johnson, Peggy A. "Be Thou My Vision." In *Speaking Out: Gifts of Ministering Undeterred by Disabilities*. Robert L. Walker, ed. Charleston: CreateSpace, Inc., 2012; 43-50.

Johnson, Peggy A. and Robert L. Walker. *Deaf Ministry: Make a Joyful Silence*. Charleston: BookSurge, Inc., 2007.

Kaye, H. Stephen, Taewoon Kang, and Mitchell P. LaPlante. "Wheelchair Use in the United States." Disability Statistics Center, Institute for Health and Aging, School of Nursing, University of California (Abstract 23), May 2002. http://dsc.ucsf.edu/publication.php.

Kessler Foundation/NOD. "The ADA, 20 Years Later." July 2010. http://www.2010disabilitysurveys.org/pdfs/surveyresults.pdf.

L'Arche. "Charter of the Communities of L'Arche. Retrieved 07/21/13. http://www.larche.org/charter-of-the-communities-of-l-arche.en-gb.43.3.content.htm.

Lauber, Melissa "Overview: Conference Adopts Bold 2020 Vision." *UM Connection–Baltimore-Washington Conference*, vol. 23, no. 6, June 13, 2012. http://www.bwcumc.org/sites/default/files/umc_pdf_files/UMC_June13_WEB.pdf.

Lewis, Hannah. *Deaf Liberation Theology*. Burlington: Ashgate Publishing Co., 2007.

Longmore, Paul K. *Why I Burned My Book and Other Essays on Disability.* Philadelphia: Temple University Press, 2003.

Marchione, Marilyn. "US Faces Surge of New Vets Seeking Disability," *Christian Science Monitor,* May 28, 2012. http://www.csmonitor.com/USA/Latest-News-Wires/2012/0528/US-faces-surge-of-new-vets-seeking-disability.

McDonald, Evelyn. "What? And She's Disabled, Too?" In *Speaking Out: Gifts of Ministering Undeterred by Disabilities.* Robert L. Walker, ed. Charleston: CreateSpace, Inc., 2012; 111-118.

McKinney, Michael. "Dancing with Shadows: Serving God in the Dim Light of Mental Illness." In *Speaking Out: Gifts of Ministering Undeterred by Disabilities.* Robert L. Walker, ed. Charleston: CreateSpace, Inc., 2012; 119-127.

Melton, Joy Thornburg. *Safe Sanctuaries: The Church Responds to Abuse, Neglect, and Exploitation of Older Adults.* Nashville: Discipleship Resources, 2012.

Mental Health Reporting. "Facts About Mental Illness and Violence." University of Washington, School of Social Work. http://depts.washington.edu/mhreport/facts_violence.php.

"Mental Illness: Facts and Numbers." National Alliance on Mental Illness. http://www.nami.org/factsheets/mentalillness_factsheet.pdf.

Multrine, Anna. "Suicide 'Epidemic' in Army: July Was Worst Month, Pentagon Says." *Christian Science Monitor,* August 17, 2012. http://www.csmonitor.com/USA/Military/2012/0817/suicide-epidemic-in-Army-July-was-worst-month-Pentagon-says.

National Alliance on Mental Illness "Mental Illness Facts and Numbers." http://www.nami.org/Template.cfm?Section=By_Illness.

National Institute on Deafness and Other Communication Disorders. "Quick Statistics." June 16, 2010. http://www.nidcd.nih.gov/health/statistics/Pages/quick.aspx.

National Association of the Deaf. "Public Accommodations." Retrieved 07/21/13. http://www.nad.org/issues/civil-rights/ada/public-accommodations.

New York Annual Conference Journal. 1997.

Newman, Gene and Joni Eareckson Tada. *All God's Children: Ministry with Disabled Persons.* Grand Rapids: Zondervan Publishing House, 1993.

Nouwen, Henri J. M. *Adam: God's Beloved.* New York: Orbis Books, 2000.

Orlando, Angie. "Poster Child." http://dotbug3.blogspot.com

Pridmore, J. Eric. "Seeing the Light: My Journey with Disability." In *Speaking Out: Gifts of Ministering Undeterred by Disabilities.* Robert L. Walker, ed. Charleston: CreateSpace, Inc., 2012; 159-167.

"Ramp Building Ministries." *The Voice of the United Methodist Disability Connection,* 1, no. 5, 2011. http://archive.constantcontact.com/fs017/1104745249463/archive/1106909966699.html.

Reinders, Hans S., ed. *The Paradox of Disability: Responses to Jean Vanier and L'Arche Communities from Theology and the Sciences.* Grand Rapids: William B. Eerdmans Publishing Company, 2010.

Reynolds, Thomas E. *Vulnerable Communion: A Theology of Disability and Hospitality.* Grand Rapids: Brazos Press, 2008.

Roberts, Lily. "We Still Aren't Meeting the Needs of Female Veterans." *Next New Deal: The Blog of the Roosevelt Institute*, March 29, 2012. http://www.nextnewdeal.net/we-still-aren%E2%80%99t-meeting-needs-female-veterans.

Roswell UMC. "Noah's Ark Sunday School Class: Ministry to the Developmentally Challenged." http://www.rumc.com/page.aspx?id=79467.

Schlintz, Victoria. "Thorns and More than Sufficient Grace." In *Speaking Out: Gifts of Ministering Undeterred by Disabilities.* Robert L. Walker, ed. Charleston: CreateSpace, Inc., 2012; 81-89.

Seymour, David T. "Life with Physical Disabilities, the Christian Life, and the Ordained Ministry." In *Speaking Out: Gifts of Ministering Undeterred by Disabilities.* Robert L. Walker, ed. Charleston: CreateSpace, Inc., 2012; 219-226.

Sharma, Elke. "Mission of Deaf Hands and Hearts." *The United Methodist Women News*, 4, No 1, 5.

Shepard, Charlotte Hawkins and Devorah Greenstein. *United Methodist Committee on Relief Accessibility Audit for Churches.* New York: UMCOR Health General Board of Global Ministries of The United Methodist Church, 2010. http://www.umdisabilityministries.org/download/auditfront.pdf.

Shepard, Charlotte, Wineva Hankamer, and Devorah Greenstein, "Communication and Etiquette with Persons with Disabilities," United Methodist Committee on DisAbility Ministries, April 2009. http://www.umdisabilityministries.org/download/10_etiquette.pdf.

Sign Enhancers, Tape #8E – "Deaf Culture Autobiography Featuring Rev. Thomas Coughlin." 1989.

Silver, Ruth. *Invisible: My Journey through Vision and Hearing Loss.* Bloomington: iUniverse, Inc., 2012.

Snider, Jan. "Church Christmas Play Stars Developmentally Disabled Adults." United Methodist News Service. December 21, 2004. http://archives.umc.org/interior.asp?ptid=2&mid=6361.

Stephen Ministries. "What Is Stephen Ministry?" 2013. http://www.stephenministries.org/stephenministry/default.cfm/917.

Stone, Cathy Capo. "Rosa Valdez Early Childhood Learning Center." *United Methodist Women News*, 4, no. 2, (2011), 7. http://new.gbgm-umc.org/umw/news/articles/item/index.cfm?id=600.

Tate, Candice M. and Scott Adams. "Information Gaps on the Deaf and Hard of Hearing Population: A Background Paper." Western Interstate Commission for Higher Education (WICHE) Mental Health Program. May 2006. www.wiche.edu/info/publications/InformationGapsResearchPaper.pdf.

Texas Council of Developmental Disabilities. "People-First Language." December 2011. http://tcdd.texas.gov/resources/people-first-language.

Tucker, Bonnie Poitras and Adam A. Milani. *Federal Disability Law in a Nutshell.* St. Paul: West Publishing Co., 1998.

"u/ability Offers Range of Spiritual Supports and Programs." *The Voice of the United Methodist Disability Connection*, 2, no.7, 2012. http://archive.constantcontact.com/fs110/1104745249463/archive/1111581677293.html

United Methodist Committee on DisAbility Ministries. "Accessibility Audits." Updated June 2013. http://www.umdisabilityministries.org/2410.html.

United Methodist Committee on DisAbility Ministries. "Learn More: Links to Resources, Organizations, and Technology." Accessed 07/21/13. http://www.umdisabilityministries.org/3000.html.

United Methodist Communications. "2010 State of the Church: Congregational Life Survey." http://www.umc.org/site/c.lwL4KnN1LtH/b.6072841/k.7ACF/2010_State_of_the_Church_Congregational_Life_Survey.htm#.Uev0tY2TiO0.

The United Methodist Hymnal. Nashville: The United Methodist Publishing House, 1989.

United States Department of Veterans Affairs. "Military Sexual Trauma." Updated August 5, 2013. http://www.womenshealth.va.gov/WOMENSHEALTH/trauma.asp.

Valentin Haüy Association. "Blindness and Visual Impairment: The Statistics." Updated July 18, 2013. http://www.avh.asso.fr/rubrics/association/statistics.php?langue=eng.

Walker, Robert L., ed. *Speaking Out: Gifts of Ministering Undeterred by Disabilities.* Charleston: CreateSpace, Inc., 2012.

Ward, Irene M. *The Ten Commandments of Communicating with People with Disabilities DVD.* New York: Program Development Associates, 2007. http://www.disabilitytraining.com.

Web, Charlie, "Eye Conditions and Disorders," 2005. http://www.99main.com/~charlief/vi/disorders.html.

World Health Organization, "Visual impairment and blindness." June 2012. http://www.who.int/mediacentre/factsheets/fs282/en/.

World Health Organization. *World Report on Disability.* Geneva, Switzerland: WHO Press, 2011.

Yong, Amos. *The Bible, Disability, and the Church: A New Vision of the People of God.* Grand Rapids: William B. Eerdmans Publishing Company, 2011.

Appendix A: Glossary

Note: Words in the text are in bold print the first time a word from the Glossary is used.

Ableism, ableist—View of the world that makes assumptions based on experiences of people who do not have disabilities; a correlate to sexism, ageism, and racism. Synonym: *Normate*.

Accessibility—Making environments useable by the greatest number of persons including people who use wheeled mobility devices, who have difficulty with hand function, who cannot see or hear well, or who are of atypical stature.

Accessibility audit—A tool and process required in the *Book of Discipline* (¶2533.6) to assess the physical environment, program, communication methods, and social climate of a congregation and determine priorities for making improvements. Some conferences have an established form to use, and others leave that up to the local church. The form used in the study is online at the UM DisAbility Committee website.

Accommodations—Individualized measures taken to allow a person who has difficulty with typical arrangements to participate in an activity such as a course or conference. Accommodations include having someone take notes, seating in the front, use of a personal FM amplification system, or taking a test orally or in a less-distracting environment. When used in ADA terminology in the phrase "reasonable accommodations," it means measures that are financially and logistically feasible. If more than one accommodation will work, the employer or school may opt for the least costly alternative.

Advocacy—Speaking or acting on behalf of a person or group that appears to have less access to power and decision making.

Assistive listening devices—Technology such as FM, infrared, or induction systems that enable persons with hearing loss to more clearly hear sounds coming from the PA system. Abbreviated ALDs, the term includes both the system and the individual receivers with headsets, earbuds, or neckloops. Some systems can be operated using the T (telecoil) switch on the listener's hearing aids.

Attitudinal barriers—Stereotypical negative thinking that automatically assumes that a person with a disability will be unable to carry out a particular task, or will demand costly modifications, or will have an intellectual disability because he or she has a physical disability.

Braille—Named for its inventor Louis Braille, a fifteen-year-old student in nineteenth-century France, this system of six raised dots is still used by many people who are born blind or lose their eyesight early in life. While some believe that digital and audio media will make Braille obsolete, others point out that unless a child learns how to spell, generate, and read words they remain functionally illiterate.

Cane-detectable—Objects and textures that a person with vision loss who uses a mobility cane can discover tactilely with the back and forth sweep of the cane tip. Examples include a floor-mounted barrier next to a protruding water fountain and edging on a pathway to make it easier to follow.

Captioning—Options of adding text to media include Real Time or live captioning; closed captioning, which is embedded in the media but must be turned on; and open captioning, which is a permanent part of the media. Automatic voice recognition captioning such as used on YouTube is not yet a valid option, as it generates many errors and often results in nonsensical sentences and phrases.

CART—Communication Access Real time Translation is a form of live captioning using court recorder technology and computer screen or projection system so that people who are Deaf and hard of hearing can follow the proceedings of a meeting or event.

CCTV magnifier—Closed circuit television magnifier, also known as a video magnifier, uses a mounted camera and television screen to zoom in on and magnify items such as a photograph, business card, recipe, or medication bottle, making it possible for persons with limited visual acuity to read and see the objects.

Cochlear implant—Technology that enables a person who is profoundly hard of hearing to be able to perceive sounds and speech when wearing a receiver that attaches magnetically to the head over a base device that has been surgically placed behind the ear. This technology was initially used for adults who had prior hearing and language skills, but is increasingly used for children who are just beginning to learn to speak. Some in the Deaf community are concerned that this technology is an assault on Deaf culture.

CODA—Child of Deaf Adults, refers to a hearing child who grows up in the Deaf community and learns ASL as his or her first language. Many CODAs become interpreters and some have difficulty fitting into the hearing world.

Communication barriers—Inaccessible technology and methods of interacting, including standard telephones, uncaptioned media, not using a PA system, or not taking the time to ensure that the listener is able to follow a conversation.

Curb cut—Also known as curb ramps, these are the sections of a curb, usually at a crosswalk, where the street level tapers to the sidewalk level for ease of use by people using wheeled mobility devices including baby strollers and bicycles in addition to wheelchairs and scooters. Newer curb cuts have an etched grid or a panel of raised dots installed in the sidewalk shortly before one reaches the street or parking lot as a cane-detectable warning that one is approaching a traffic area.

Deaf—When spelled with a capital "D", Deaf denotes people who have partial or complete hearing loss, use American Sign Language (ASL), and identify with Deaf culture. In contrast to using people-first language, many Deaf individuals refer to themselves as Deaf people, not persons who are Deaf.

Deaf community—Persons who identify with Deaf culture and are fluent in ASL or the indigenous sign language of the country where they reside.

Deaf culture—Considered a subculture within the US because it has its own language (ASL), literature, ways of interacting, and clear sense of identity. Much of the culture was passed down by teachers and older students at state-run boarding schools for Deaf children. Even when sign language was forbidden, it lived as an underground language, which further intensified the sense of belonging to a special group.

Deaf-blind—Persons who are both legally blind and have significant hearing loss; some have complete visual loss and deafness, for example, Helen Keller.

Disability—A very broad term that refers to a physical, intellectual, or emotional condition that limits being able to carry out at least some everyday activities in a standard fashion. The term can refer to a category of supplemental income for people who meet the criteria and find themselves unable to work, but also to people who find ways to work full time and to live independent, productive lives. Because of the stigma attached to the word, many people who have major limitations in daily activities never consider themselves to have a disability.

Disability awareness—Activities done to sensitize able-bodied people as to what living with a disability entails, common barriers that people with a disability face, and what people with disabilities are able to achieve and contribute.

Disability community—Usually used to describe persons with lifelong or early acquired disabilities who self-identify as having a disability and self-advocate for needed societal changes. Members of this community may consider it a subculture. Examples of disability culture include magazines by and for people with disabilities, the academic field of disability studies, and various artistic expressions by persons with disabilities.

Disability ministry—This term finds broad use in churches, ranging from segregated ministries to and for people with disabilities, to inclusive ministries with and by people with disabilities.

Disability theology—A branch of liberation theology that looks at Christianity from the perspective of marginalized people, placing them in the center of the dialogue as Jesus did. Nancy Eiesland's book *The Disabled God* is perhaps the seminal work in this field. The book argues that Jesus, with his wounds and loss of mobility as he was dying on the cross, understands what it is like to have a disability and that in him God became disabled.

Empowerment—A term to be used carefully, as it implies that one group has the power and is able to decide who else can receive power to control their own lives. In its best sense, the word implies finding ways for people with disabilities to be brought into the center of decision making.

Etiquette—Disability etiquette describes ways of interacting respectfully and appropriately with persons who have disabilities.

Full participation—Achieved when persons with disabilities are completely involved in the life of the organization, for instance using one's gifts to serve as lay speakers, committee chairs, choir leaders, soloists, cooks, or in any other such role. It also means that people with disabilities have friends and outside relationships within an organization to the same extent as people without disabilities do. Synonyms: *Integration, Full Inclusion.*

Halo effect—The tendency to put a person with a disability on a pedestal and offer disproportionate praise for accomplishing activities that typical individuals do, because of a biased assumption that people with disabilities aren't capable.

Handicap—An outdated term for what we now call disability. See the text for a history of the word (Chapter 3).

Handicapist—An attitude that limits expectations for people with disabilities. Considering people with disabilities as conditions to be fixed or charity recipients to be served would be examples of this attitude.

Handicapping conditions—Environmental or social conditions that prevent a person with a disability from full participation in activities of their choice. Synonyms: *Architectural* and *attitudinal barriers.*

Hearing community—This community consists of persons who use spoken language as their primary means of communication. They may happen to have a profound hearing loss but not be interested in learning sign language. Deaf children of hearing parents may grow up very isolated in the hearing community because those around them do not make the effort to communicate.

Hidden disability—A condition that limits a person's ability to carry out everyday activities, but is not visible to others. Hidden disabilities include cardiac and respiratory limitations, multiple chemical sensitivities, chronic back pain, mild head injuries, seizure disorders, and more.

Inclusion—Being involved in the same activity at the same time as typical peers, even though the activity may be in modified form for the person with a disability.

Integration—A step beyond inclusion, where a person with a disability is not only invited to participate and be physically present, but is fully involved in all aspects of the activity and community, including leadership and friendship. Synonyms: *Full participation, full inclusion.*

Late-deafened—Also called deaf with a small "d", this term relates to a person who, after language acquisition in childhood or later, had a significant hearing loss that can't be adequately corrected by hearing aids. Most late-deafened adults do not learn sign language and rely on captioning and other technology.

Lip-reading—Also known as speech-reading, this is the skill of being able to comprehend spoken language by watching the speaker's mouth and facial expressions. This works best to supplement residual hearing and when the listener understands the context, as only 30 to 40 percent of spoken English can be detected visually.

Normate—A perspective through which one looks at things assuming they pertain to people who do not have disabilities. For instance, one would assume that literature is written by and to be read by people without disabilities. Any character with a disability would be discussed from the viewpoint of a person without a disability. Synonym: *Ableist.*

Orientation and mobility skills—Specialized skill training for people who are blind, including learning to walk with a mobility cane or Guide Dog, ride public transportation, and pay attention to traffic and other environmental cues in order to independently navigate throughout the community.

Parish nurse—A specially trained registered nurse who functions as a church staff person and assists members and the parish through integrating faith and health. Specifically, parish nurses advocate and make referrals, set up support groups, provide health education and counseling, and coordinate volunteers to meet assessed needs in the congregation. Also known as faith community nurse.

People-first language—A respectful way of always naming the person first and never referring to a person or group of people by their condition. Examples include: Joe, who has had a stroke; the boy who has Down syndrome; the woman who is blind. Better yet is referring to people by their names, not mentioning the disability unless there is a need to do so. Negative images like "wheelchair bound" (use "a person who uses a wheelchair" instead) or "suffering from" a condition are avoided. Also referred to as person-first language.

Pew cut—The space left when the ends of one or preferably two adjacent sanctuary pews are cut shorter so that a person using a wheelchair can sit in the midst of the congregation next to her or his companions.

Good planning offers choices and ensures a line of vision when a person in the space is seated and other congregants are standing.

Platform lift—A form of moving a person (and her or his mobility device if the person uses one) between levels (for example, from the sanctuary floor to the chancel area) by means of a lift that raises and lowers vertically or at an angle. The latter is called an incline platform lift. Lifts can be encased or open, moveable or fixed. They cost significantly less than elevators.

Respite—In the church, this refers to programming to allow parents of children with disabilities to have some time off while the children are in a safe, volunteer-run program, which is usually scheduled once or twice a month for several hours. This term also refers to programs for older adults with dementia, which similarly provide a few hours for self-care and personal activities for caregivers.

Self-advocacy—Often used to describe training given to youth or young adults with an intellectual or developmental disability so they learn how to explain and request accommodations needed in order to succeed. The training usually includes skills for community access, communication, and safety to enable a successful transition into the post-school world.

Stephen Ministries—A congregational program involving laypersons who undertake specialized training and receive ongoing supervision to enable them to support individuals or families in crisis.

Stigma—A set of negative perceptions based on an identity or condition over which a person has no control. Fear of being labeled and embarrassed causes many to try to hide their own condition or that of a loved one. Mental illness is perhaps the most frequently stigmatized condition in the US.

Temporarily able-bodied—A person who does not currently have a disability, abbreviated as TAB; a term coined in the disability community to make the point that many people will acquire a temporary or permanent disability in the course of their lifetime.

TTY—Text telephones, also known as TDD (or telecommunications device for the deaf), offer a form of telephone communication that is rapidly declining due to the increased use of videophones and mobile telephone text messaging. Users type messages back and forth, but at a slower rate than texting or chatting on a social media site.

Vulnerable adults—Usually used in connection with Safe Sanctuaries volunteer training and screening policies, this refers to any adult eighteen and over who has an intellectual or cognitive disability and needs assistance with decision making and safety. While this category is not a legal one, a church would do well to use a broad interpretation of this status in assigning volunteers and carrying out programs. One should presume competency in interacting with any adult, but follow Safe Sanctuary guidelines in all disability programming.

Lynn Swedberg, MS, OTR/L
Disability Consultant and Newsletter Editor
United Methodist Committee on DisAbility
Ministries (www.umdisabilityministries.org).**United Methodist Women Connections and Resources**

Appendix B: Resources

National mission institutions supported by United Methodist Women mission giving:

Camp Aldersgate, Little Rock, Arkansas—Provides summer camping and weekend respite camps for children with disabilities and medical conditions: http://www.campaldersgate.net

Cunningham Children's Home, Urbana, Illinois—Offers special education and schooling to students with a variety of disabilities, primarily emotional/behavioral difficulties: http://www.cunninghamhome.org

Epworth Children & Family Services, St. Louis, Missouri—Provides stable housing and education for youth with severe emotional, mental, or behavioral issues: http://www.epworth.org

MacDonell's Children's Home, Houma, Louisiana—Residential facility for male youth with a history of severe abuse and resulting behavioral and emotional needs: http://www.macdonellchildren.org

Rural Mission & Wesley Centers, Atlanta, Georgia—Offers home repairs for adults who have disabilities and/or are elderly: http://www.wesleycenters.org/

International ministries projects supported by United Methodist Women mission giving:

1. Yekaterinburg, Russia, Club Hope. Helps keep children with disabilities in the community by providing rehabilitation and education resources. See http://new.gbgm-umc.org/umw/resources/articles/item/index.cfm?id=955.

2. Lahore, Pakistan: Church of Pakistan—Dar-ul-Mussarat Lahore Center for Mentally Challenged. The Center trains students to become as independent as possible and works with awareness raising to increase acceptance. Funding provided for the lunch program, which is part of the training in basic skills for living.

3. Montevideo, Uruguay: Methodist Church of Uruguay—Skills and employment program for youth with disabilities. Youth are taught the skills to manufacture clothing and accessories.

4. Yekaterinburg, Russia, in partnership with Christian Women—Technologies for Disabled Children and Their Parents (2011 grant). This project provides training activities for preschool and young school children with physical and developmental disabilities and their parents. Funds were contributed to purchase media equipment.

Special opportunity to give:

United Methodist Women's Mission Giving supports partners and programs in disability ministries.

You can give toward these programs via project #3019230 Disability Programs, a supplementary giving opportunity. United Methodist Women members are encouraged to give through regular giving channels and note the funds are for the Disabilities Projects #3019230 Disability Programs. You can also send checks directly to the national office. Please make them payable to "United Methodist Women" with the project name and number in the memo section.

Your giving makes a difference.

Deaconesses and home missioners engaged in ministries with persons with disabilities:

Charmaine Cothran, deaconess, Chicago, Illinois; Northern Illinois Annual Conference, Founder and director of African Americans Living with Multiple Sclerosis.

Vae Rose Fultz, deaconess, Jacksonville, Illinois; Illinois Great Rivers Annual Conference Jacksonville UM Deaf Faith Community.

Leslie J. Hobson, deaconess, Brainerd, Minnesota; Minnesota Annual Conference Integration Specialist Coordinator, Minnesota Conference Retreats & Camping Office.

Cynthia Andrade Johnson, deaconess, Brownsville, Texas; Rio Grande Annual Conference. Special education teacher in the Brownsville Independent School.

M. Cameron Kempson, deaconess, Arden, North Carolina; Western North Carolina Annual Conference SimplyHome-CMI, Client Care Specialist.

Gladis Lobato, deaconess, Brooklyn, New York; New York Annual Conference Habilitation Assistant, United Cerebral Palsy of NYC.

Robin Minick, deaconess, Waynesville, North Carolina; Holston Annual Conference Mental and Behavioral Health Clinician, Appalachian Community Services.

Barbara Skarbowski, deaconess, Lancaster, Pennsylvania; Eastern Pennsylvania Annual Conference Chair, Eastern Pennsylvania Conference Committee on Disability Concerns. Secretary, United Methodist Committee on DisAbility Ministries.

M. Scott Vickery, home missioner, Greater New Jersey Annual Conference Executive Secretary for Community Relations, United Methodist Women National Office. Previously, Special Education teacher.

For information on how to contact the above and a complete list of others in disability ministries, please call the Offices of Deaconess, Home Missioner, and Home Missionary: 212-870-3580.

Additional United Methodist Women resources:

Spanish translation of *The Church and People with Disabilities* by Peggy A. Johnson
ISBN: 978-1-940182-01-8
M3183
$10

Korean translation of *The Church and People with Disabilities* by Peggy A. Johnson
ISBN: 978-1-940182-02-5
M3184
$10

response magazine, May 2014, focusing on the church and people with disabilities

Place your order with:
United Methodist Women Mission Resources
1-800-357-9857
www.umwmissionresources.org

The Church and People with Disabilities webpage: www.unitedmethodistwomen.org/disabilities

Other United Methodist disability resources:

Annual Conferences with Disability Committees, http://www.umdisabilityministries.org/3100.html

United Methodist Association of Ministers with Disabilities, http://www.umdisabledministers.org/

United Methodist Committee on Deaf and Hard of Hearing Ministries, http://www.umcdhm.org/

United Methodist Committee on DisAbility Ministries, http://www.umdisabilityministries.org

United Nations' webpage on disabilities:

http://www.un.org/disabilities/default.asp?id=150

About the Author

Peggy A. Johnson is the bishop of the Philadelphia Area of The United Methodist Church and was elected to the episcopacy in 2008. She is a native of Baltimore, Maryland, where she served in the Baltimore-Washington Conference as an elder since 1981. She received her education from Lebanon Valley College (BS), Asbury Theological Seminary (M.Div.), and Wesley Theological Seminary (D.Min.). She has served a number of United Methodist congregations, including the historic Christ United Methodist Church of the Deaf. She is married to Rev. Michael C. Johnson and the Johnsons have two adult sons, Peter and Gabriel.